MITCHAM HISTORIES: 10

RAVENSBURY

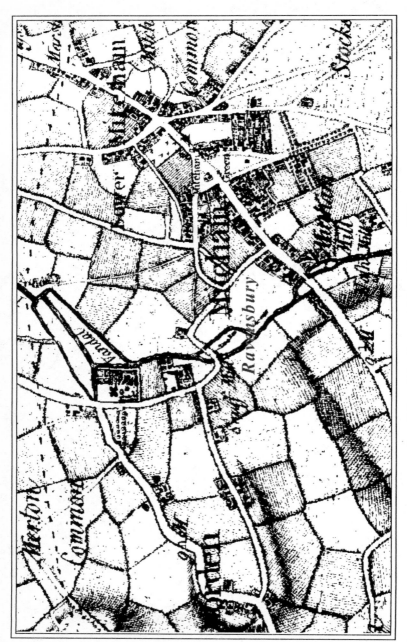

Detail from John Rocque's Map of Surrey 1768

MITCHAM HISTORIES: 10

RAVENSBURY

E N MONTAGUE

MERTON HISTORICAL SOCIETY

Published by

MERTON HISTORICAL SOCIETY

2008

© E N Montague 2008

ISBN 978 1 903899 56 4

Printed by intypelibra

PREFACE

For historical reasons, to be explored in Chapter I, the manor of Ravensbury extended, albeit in a piecemeal fashion, to various parts of the ancient ecclesiastical parishes of Mitcham and Morden. For the purposes of this study, however, 'Ravensbury' is considered in the main as that part of Lower Mitcham lying on the north or right bank of the river Wandle between Mitcham Bridge and Morden Hall Park, and bounded on the north by Morden Road, but also includes a large area to the south extending as far as Central Road.

Within this area is the site of one of the largest 'Dark Age' cemeteries known in southern England, the early collective burial place of the community to whose descendants by 1086 this part of Surrey had become known as Michelham.

In the Middle Ages two large houses occupied choice sites by the waterside, one the manor house of Ravensbury itself, and the other the 'messuage' of one of the premier families in Surrey. Over a period of six centuries a succession of houses here were to be the country residences of government officials and city merchants, bankers and industrialists, each of whom made his own contribution to the life of the village outside their gates.

The houses have now vanished, and with them the textile printing industry and snuff and tobacco manufactory for which the area was once renowned. Although pollution of its water has rendered the Wandle unable to sustain the trout for which it was at one time famous, the river still provides a visually attractive feature through Ravensbury Park, linking the National Trust's Watermeads property with the extensive grounds of Morden Hall.

Much of the history of Ravensbury has already appeared in print, though in a variety of forms. Thus in 1959 Surrey Archaeological Society, in volume LVI of its *Collections*, published the definite study of the Anglo-Saxon Cemetery at Mitcham by Lt.-Col. H. F. Bidder and John Morris. In 1973 far smaller excavations than those conducted by Bidder prompted the publication of *The Ravensbury Story* by the London Borough of Merton Parks, Cemeteries and Allotments Department, for which I supplied the text – and in 1981 an improved version was the subject of a booklet, *Ravensbury Manor House and Park*, published by Merton Historical Society. In April and May 1974 The *Merton Borough News* serialised over a period of six weeks the history of Mitcham Grove, a collaborative study for which biographical work on the Hoare and Lubbock families was undertaken by a fellow member of Merton Historical Society, the late Doris E. Dawes. Five years later *Ravensbury* was the subject of Merton Town Trails leaflet number 6, published by the Merton Town Trails Association in 1979. A general absence of anything readily available for the student on one of the most important of the Wandle-based industries prompted me to write *Textile Bleaching and Printing in Mitcham and Merton 1590-1870*, which was published by the Libraries Department of the London Borough of Merton in 1992. This contains a chapter expressly devoted to the pioneering Ravensbury printing works, which functioned from the late 17th century until collapse of the industry locally in the 1860s. Also in 1992 *The Wandle Trail* was published by The Wandle Industrial Museum, containing as Walk 2 a revised version of two unfortunately inaccurate booklets the Museum produced a few years previously. Finally, in 1995 Merton Historical Society published, in the same format as its earlier booklet, the history of *The Ravensbury Mills*.

None of the foregoing, however, dealt with the history of Ravensbury as a coherent whole, although the material was available in typescript. For several years it had been obvious that constant updating and revision of much of my original texts, quite apart from the fact that they were not indexed, had rendered them virtually useless for reference purposes. It therefore seemed pressing, having completed in 1994 a comprehensive updating of my material on Lower Mitcham, to continue the process by bringing together the notes on Ravensbury in one volume. What follows is the result.

The maps and illustrations chosen are by no means all that are available. They have been selected partly because they were readily to hand, but mainly to add some interest to the text and, above all, to assist the reader unfamiliar with the locality. In a few instances, such as detailed accounts of the various premises, including the Ravensbury print works, offered for sale in 1855, abridgement has been necessary in the interest of producing a balanced and, it is hoped, readable account.

Given the unevenness of the source material, and the pitfalls of inadequate understanding and inadvertent bias, the compilation of a history such as this has, perforce, to be a compromise. There is certainly a considerable amount of biographical data available on some of the personalities mentioned – Doris Dawes, for instance, found herself embarrassed by a surfeit of riches – and yet of others we have so little information. The archives of Hoare's Bank will, no doubt, contain much information on 'Henry of Mitcham' which could be fascinating, and the family records of the Bidder family are another source, although here E F Clark's biography of his great-grandfather *George Parker Bidder, The Calculating Boy*, has done much to place this in the public domain.

The result of research conducted over a period of some 40 years, this study inevitably derives much from the scholarship of others, which I acknowledge with gratitude. Doris Dawes has been mentioned already, and I am also much indebted to the late Winifred Mould, another member of Merton Historical Society, and to William Prentis for information on the snuff milling industry. Where I have drawn from published sources these have been quoted as a matter of course, but regrettably I am unable to mention by name the archivists and librarians whose assistance over the years proved invaluable. To them collectively I say "thank you". I am also indebted to friends like Lionel Green, whose information about the Norman landowners was so useful, and to Judith Goodman without whose help the agriculturist John Arbuthnot would have received only the briefest of mention. The sections by Bill Rudd, David Bird and Peter Hopkins have added immeasurably to the value of this study, which has evolved very much as collaborative effort. I thank most sincerely those members of our 'editorial sub-committee' who read through my earlier text and gently drew attention to those stupid mistakes, be they in spelling or syntax, which might otherwise have slipped through unnoticed until it was too late to alter them. Finally I thank Peter Hopkins for his expertise in preparing this tenth volume in the Society's 'Mitcham Histories' ready for the printers.

E N Montague   October 2008

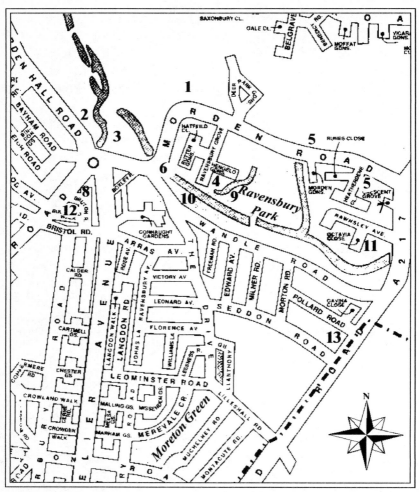

1 **White Cottage**   2 **Morden Lodge (Growtes)**
3 **Little Steelhaws**   4 **Ravensbury Print Works (site)**
5 **'Dark Age' Cemetery**   6 **Ravensbury Mills**
7 **Grove House (site)**   8 **The Grange (Steelhawes)**
9 **Old Ravensbury Manor House (site)** 10 **Ravensbury Barn (site)**
11 **Mitcham Grove (site)**   12 **Morden Farm (site)**
13 **'Ravensbury Manor' (site'**

Detail from a modern street map, showing the area covered by this book.
Reproduced by permission of Merton Design Unit, London Borough of Merton

CONTENTS

MAPS AND ILLUSTRATIONS

Imperial Measures are used in most sections of this book
1 acre = 4 roods = 160 square rods, poles or perches = 0.4047 hectares
1 yard = 3 feet = 0.9144 metres
1 mile = 1.61 kilometres
1 ton = 20 cwt = 80 quarters = 2240 lb (pounds) = 1.016 tonnes
£1 = 20s (shillings) = 240d (pence)
1 gallon = 4.5 litres
1 (British) horse power = 0.746 Kw

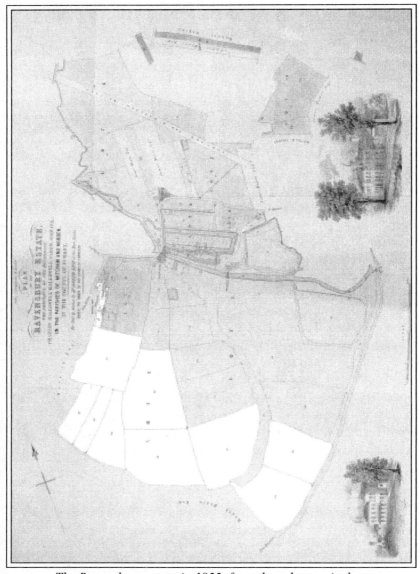

*The Ravensbury estate in 1855, from the sales particulars
reproduced by courtesy of Surrey History Service
The Grange (Steelhawes) is depicted at the bottom left hand corner and a
sketch of old Ravensbury manor house is on the right.*

THE MANOR OF RAVENSBURY

Origins

The origins of the manor of Ravensbury appear to lie in two small estates within what later became the ecclesiastical parish of Mitcham.[1] One, which included a water-mill, was in Lower Mitcham, or Whitford, probably on the right or north bank of the Wandle in the vicinity of the ford by which the river was crossed. At the time of Edward the Confessor this was held by a Saxon named Lank or Lang. Until the Norman Conquest the other holding was in the possession of another Saxon, Ledmer or Lemar, and seems to have been located downstream from the ford. This second estate can best be identified with the area now known as Ravensbury, centred on Ravensbury Park, and lying between the Wimbledon to Croydon tramway and the Wandle.

At the time of the Domesday survey in 1086 Whitford – the spelling varies considerably[2] – was recognised as a separate 'vill' or settlement within the hundred of Wallington, but as a distinct locality it virtually disappears from the documentary record sometime in the later Middle Ages. Wickford mill, immediately upstream from the ford and presumably the successor to a watermill owned by Lank, finds mention as late as 1654.[3] To the north the 'vill', or hamlet, probably extended as far as the Lower Green, the eastern half of which was still referred to as 'Whitford Green' in the 19th century although, paradoxically, it actually fell within the jurisdiction of the manor of Vauxhall.

Prior to the Conquest Lank's holding had been assessed for tax purposes on the basis of two hides, indicating an area of perhaps 240 acres, and the whole estate was worth 50 shillings, a substantial proportion of which was probably attributable to the mill. Even if one makes allowance for the income from milling, however, this valuation was comparatively high, and suggests that Lank's land was in the main on the rich alluvial soil to be found overlying the terrace gravels of the Wandle flood plain. As one might expect in these circumstances, much of Lank's holding was arable, and in 1086, when he was no longer in possession, it was worked by one plough shared between the two villeins or smallholders on the estate, whilst another was kept on the demesne, or home farm.

Lank also held 24 acres of meadow, which is likely to have comprised permanent grassland on the banks of the river, where it was vulnerable to seasonal flooding.[4]

Of Lank himself we can say relatively little. A tenant-in-chief of the King, he would have been a freeholder, perhaps holding his land by title deed and exempt from most duties other than the three public charges of military service, bridge repair and the building of fortifications. He is mentioned in the Surrey folios of Domesday Book only in relation to his holding in Whitford and, presumably suffering the fate of many Saxon thegns with Harold's defeat at Hastings, lost his land, if not his life.

By 1086 Lank's former holding in Whitford was in the hands of William Fitz Ansculf or fitzAnsculf, son of Ansculf de Picquigny, to whom it had been granted by the Conqueror. De Picquigny was one of the great Norman landowners, and had been appointed sheriff of Surrey by about 1071.[5] Of his very considerable possessions in the gift of the king (he held 86 English manors), the principal was the castle at Dudley, in the Midlands.[6] He was also the sheriff of Buckinghamshire, where the majority of his holdings were to be found. By the time Domesday was compiled, Ansculf de Picquigny was dead, but most, if not all, of his Surrey estates, amongst which were Wandsworth, and his holdings in Mitcham and Whitford, had passed to his son William. Shortly before the survey of 1086 tenure of the Whitford estate had been granted by Fitz Ansculf to another of the king's Norman followers, William the Chamberlain, a Frenchman from Tancarville, a small town at the mouth of the Seine near Le Havre.

Soon after 1066 the value of the Whitford holding fell from 50 to 22 shillings, and by 1086 the basis for assessment had been halved to one hide. Within these 20 years, however, the estate as a whole had more than recovered its former value, perhaps under the direct management of William the Chamberlain or a new, responsible, tenant living at the home farm, for when the Domesday survey was conducted it was worth 60 shillings. These changes are difficult to explain, but the halving of the assessment ("then it answered for 2 hides, now for 1 hide") does imply that the holding may have been reduced in size over the intervening years. To speculate further, an explanation for the sharp drop in value soon after the Conquest could lie in the fortunes of Lank's watermill. Neglect of essential maintenance, fire or even malicious damage during the immediate post-1066 upheaval could have left the mill temporarily out of action, and therefore of little or no value. Two decades later, apparently once more in full working order and proving an asset, it was valued by the king's commissioners at 20 shillings.

Downstream from the mill, Ledmer's land which, like that of Lank, was held directly from King Edward, was assessed for taxation purposes on the basis of two and a quarter hides. It was deemed to be worth 40 shillings, and included a half share in a second mill valued at 20 shillings. Ledmer would also have ranked as a minor thegn and, like Lank, is likely to have been a franklin or freeholder, able to demonstrate his title by formal deed.

Ledmer is not recorded in Domesday as owning land in any other part of Surrey, but he may have had estates elsewhere in the kingdom, for there is no indication that demesne lands were included in his Mitcham holding. On the other hand, since the survey was conducted 20 years after the Conquest, it is possible that his Mitcham homestead had been 'wasted' and left derelict, the holding losing its identity in the intervening years and being absorbed into the larger estate held by Fitz Ansculf or William the Chamberlain. The fact that Ledmer had a half interest in another mill points to his lands having extended downstream as far as Phipps Bridge, where a second watermill, 'Pippesmulle', was working in the mid-13th century. With the estate's relatively high valuation, even after a deduction is made for the mill, it seems a reasonable assumption that Ledmer's land, like that owned by Lank upstream, was on the deep loams overlying the terrace gravels. In Ledmer's case this could well have included a substantial area of the 'Blacklands', the west common field of Mitcham, which extended as far as Phipps Bridge and included a substantial portion of what many years later became the Morden Hall estate.

As we have seen, William Fitz Ansculf's Whitford property included the home farm on Lank's former holding. Here, we might expect, his bailiff lived. With its productive arable land and 24 acres of waterside meadow – a valuable source of winter fodder as well as being used for summer grazing – the farm should have been productive and profitable.

One of the estate tenants would most likely have been the miller, and the little community of peasants should have been largely self-sufficient.

The 1086 survey shows Fitz Ansculf had not sub-let the adjoining Ravensbury holding, which may by this time have been run as part of a larger estate extending beyond the river to the south. The hidal assessment of the Mitcham property had remained unchanged since the reign of King Edward but, like Lank's former holding, it had evidently suffered neglect, for it was only worth 13 shillings and four pence when Fitz Ansculf's father received it from the Conqueror. The tenantry in 1086 included two villeins, who would each have had their smallholdings, probably including strips in the common field, and six 'cottars' or cottagers. If we are correct in the belief that the estate lay downstream from Whitford, we can visualise the tenantry living in a cluster of dwellings, perhaps alongside Ravensbury Lane, the bridleway leading from Mitcham to Morden, and close by the point where the lane crossed the river in what is now Ravensbury Park. It was here that medieval pottery sherds were recovered during excavations in 1973,[7] and where

The Wandle at Ravensbury – undated watercolour by William Wood Fenning (1799-1872), whose grandfather and father were proprietors of the printworks, possibly during an 1850 visit, reproduced by courtesy of Sue Wilmott

the manor house of Ravensbury stood during the Tudor period. The archaeological evidence certainly points to the site having been a focus of settlement for a very long time. However, it is most unlikely that Ansculf or his son would have maintained lodgings here or, indeed, anywhere else on their small Mitcham estates, although the riverside setting was pleasant enough. Far better accommodation would have been available in London and elsewhere on their more substantial properties when business brought them to England.

Eventually much of Fitz Ansculf's extensive property, and many of his titles, were inherited by a descendant, Roger de Sumery[8] (or 'Sumeri') and, early in the 12th century, we find Alexander de Witford, or 'Wykford', holding land in Mitcham for a knight's fee of the honour of Dudley and the barony of de Sumery.[9] Clearly, on this evidence, some subdivision of Ansculf's Lower Mitcham estate had taken place, and before he died in 1129 William the Chamberlain had been allowed to grant a sub-tenancy of his Whitford holding to another Norman noble, Laurence de Sancto Sepulchro of Rouen, who held the manor of Ashtead.[10]

If the picture locally is a little confusing, nationally the situation was certainly fluid, if not verging on the chaotic. Henry I had defeated his brother Robert and the rebellious Norman barons at the battle of Tenchebrai in 1106, and with his nephew Henry de Blois, a Cluniac monk and papal legate, installed as bishop of Winchester, he eventually established control of the Church by insisting on oaths of fealty and homage from newly invested prelates. By dint of his strong personality and his undertaking to uphold the laws of Edward the Confessor (as modified by William I) Henry gained the support of the English. Following the death of his son in the *White Ship* disaster, Henry's efforts to secure the succession of his family through his daughter Matilda did not meet with immediate success, although the Crown did eventually pass to his grandson. On Henry's death in 1135 the throne was seized by his nephew and protégé Stephen de Blois, and for the next 19 years the country was plunged into civil war whilst the barons, divided by their loyalties, fought for one side or the other. Order unfortunately did not return with the death of Stephen and the accession in 1154 of Henry II. The new king soon found himself embroiled in renewed conflict with his turbulent

barons, and his efforts to assert his authority over the Church resulted
in the murder at Canterbury of his former companion Thomas Becket,
the London merchant's son who had received his early education at
Merton priory.

Laurence of Rouen had considerable interests in London and the Home
Counties, much of which would eventually have passed to his son Robert.
The latter, however, seems to have died childless sometime before 1183,
and his sister Mary therefore inherited the Mitcham property, which
she and her husband Ralph Fitz Robert of Rouen continued to hold
under William the Chamberlain's son. Mary also inherited the manor of
Ashtead. William Chamberlain of Tancarville (grandson of Fitz Ansculf's
tenant, the first William the Chamberlain) in his turn granted the
Ravensbury property to William de Mara and Lettice (or 'Lecia') his
wife, who was the daughter and heiress of Ralph and Mary.[11] Tenure
was subject to the same conditions and feudal services observed by
their predecessors under William of Tancarville's father and grandfather.
A charter of Henry II, datable to between 1180 and 1183, confirmed
the transfer of title and also the granting of Ashtead (or 'Esteda') by
William Chamberlain of Tancarville to William de Mara for £6 p.a. "for
all services". By a deed of between *c.*1191 and 1200, perhaps in 1197,
Ralf the Chamberlain of Tancarville confirmed the transfer of the land
at Mitcham, Ashtead, Harlaxton and Londonthorpe, Lincs, to Lecia's
son, William de Mara or 'de la Mare' to hold at a rent of four marks.[12]

The place-name Ravensbury was seen by Gover *et al* as a late burh-
name with Raf or Ralph as the first element.[13] In this case, they submitted,
'bury' may have been used in the later manorial sense rather than that
of a fortified place. The Raf or Ralph who might have given his name to
the emerging manor has not been identified. The name was not
uncommon, but it is tempting to suggest either Ralph FitzRobert of Rouen
or Ralph the Chamberlain of Tancarville as a candidate, but this must
remain pure speculation.

The de Whitford family meantime were proving themselves benefactors
of the Church. In addition to the property granted by de Sumery early in
the 12th century, they were in possession of other land in Lower Mitcham,
and Richard de Whitford granted "the land which is called

Wihtrichescrofte", plus an acre of common land and an acre of demesne, together with other plots totalling six acres, to the priory of St Mary at Southwark some time between 1110 and 1130. As it transpired, these would form the nucleus of an estate the priory was to hold in Mitcham until the Dissolution.[14] (Interestingly, part of the land which John de Whitford confirmed having given to the priory sometime before 1170 was intended specifically to secure an income for the provision of candles for the church of St Peter at Mitcham – the first hint we have of the existence of a church in the village).[15] During the reign of Henry III (i.e. sometime after 1216) another Alexander de Wickford, probably representing the third generation, is recorded as holding 'a fee' (i.e. land which could be inherited and carried no manorial obligations) in Mitcham of the honour of Dudley,[16] and in 1218-19 he conveyed to Henry Cresby and his wife Alice land carrying the obligation to find one third of a knight's fee.[17] This, surely, was the same Alexander de Whitford who, in a deed dated to between 1200 and 1230, acknowledged the tithes of his corn and mill to be the right of Southwark priory.[18] Another member of the family is mentioned in the *Victoria County History*, which adds that "later" (i.e. after 1218-19) "William Mareys enfeoffed Arnold de Wickford of a messuage in Mitcham and 17 acres of land".[19] This would appear to be the estate in Lower Mitcham within the manor of Ravensbury which was still owned by the Mareys, Mareis, de Mara or de la Mare family (the variations in spelling are legion) in the 14th century.

Rouen, the principal town of Normandy, had close ties with England since the Conquest, and was a stronghold of loyalty to King John in his struggle with Phillip II of France to retain the Angevin inheritance. After their initial success at Mirabeaux in 1202 the English suffered continuous defeats, and with resistance in the rest of the duchy having collapsed by 1203, the citizens of Rouen surrendered. The severance of England from Normandy was complete.

The de Mara Dynasty

Throughout the 13th, and for part of the 14th, centuries the powerful de Mara family, lords of the manor of Ashtead, were in possession of not only the lordship of Ravensbury and the original Domesday holdings,[1] but also a large estate extending from Lower Mitcham into Morden and as far as Colliers Wood. They are said to have had an interest in a corn mill on the Wandle at Merton, belonging to the archbishop of Canterbury as part of his manor of Mortlake.[2] Early 19th-century deeds and sale particulars disclose that numerous properties in Mitcham, notably to the east of both Upper and Lower Greens, were also copyholds of the manor of Ravensbury, although it seems unlikely they had been part of the original manor. Between 1217 and 1226 William 'de la Mare' was deputy sheriff of Surrey to William de Warenne, earl of Surrey,[3] and was appointed an assize commissioner in 1223. A most experienced local government official – the Exchequer dealt with him as if he was in fact sheriff – in 1225 Sir William was party to a 'convention' with the abbot of Westminster and the prior of Merton concerning the closure of an ancient highway in Morden. It was agreed that a new 12-feet-wide diversion should be constructed, described as a "common way for men on horse or on foot and for carts leading from the corner of the abbot's court at Morden north-west to the south corner of the tenement next to the house of William, son of Sweyn".[4] The location of the manor house of de Mara's estate has not been established, but a site to the south of today's Morden Hall Park, in which what could have been a moat has been identified,[5] is a possibility.

Sir William died in 1235.[6] Another William de Mara, or de la Mare, is said to have been holding the lordship of the manor of Ravensbury in 1250,[7] but this is based on a mistake by Lysons, followed blindly by later writers. The document he quotes is that of 1225 above. There is no reference to Ravensbury in the original document, but a late 14th- or early 15th-century scribe has added a marginal note: "The same William de Mara was lord of Ravesbury". The name 'Rasebury' is otherwise first found in a Feet of Fines for 1377, and 'Ravesbury' in a document of 1488.[8] The estate seems to have undergone division, for Heales noted in his *Records of Merton Priory* that *c.*1242, a "Sir Matthew de la Mare" made a gift to Merton priory of nine acres of land which he owned in Mitcham, together with buildings and appurtenances.[9] By 1283 tenure had passed to a John "De la Mar" who, with his wife Petronill(a), in that year received a coveted grant of free warren, i.e. the right to take and preserve game, including fish, on their demesne lands in

Mitcham.[10] As was customary upon the demise of one of the king's tenants-in-chief, when John died in 1314 an *inquisition post mortem* was held not only to establish formally the identity and age of the heir, but also the extent of the lands making up the estate. The enquiry confirmed John to be in possession of the manor in the right of his daughter Florence, who held the manor "peaceably", i.e. free from disturbance, for six years during the life of her mother, Petronilla. On Florence's behalf, as a token of fealty, John had rendered annually a pair of gilt spurs worth sixpence to Peter de Montfort, lord of Ashtead and a cousin by marriage.[11] To the manor itself belonged the home farm and demesne lands, comprising 110 acres of arable, 23 acres of meadow, a watermill, and other property bringing in rents totalling 8 marcs. In addition, de la Mare held 60 acres of arable and 12 of meadow "outside the manor" – possibly in Colliers Wood – as a tenant of Henry Pas, Lord of Barnack,[12] successor in title to William Fitz Ansculf, plus another parcel of land for which he paid homage to the prior of Merton.[13] Following the death of John de la Mare (Manning and Bray describe him as "de Bradewell") lordship of the manor and tenure of the estates passed to Florence, his heiress.[12]

The broad similarity of the demesne lands of Ravensbury and the Domesday holding of William the Chamberlain in 1086 suggests that in extent it had probably remained substantially the same property. Further acquisitions of land over the passage of the next 200 years were to enlarge the estate very considerably, and with it the jurisdiction claimed and exercised by successive lords of the manor. Eventually copyholds were enfranchised and the manor declined in importance and value until the final extinguishing of feudal dues early in the 20th century.

Although of course one cannot be certain, it does seem likely that the site of the de la Mares' mill, mentioned in the enquiry of 1314, was a little upstream from the point where the Wandle is crossed today by the road to Sutton. Once a river had been brought under control and a mill pond constructed, it would be logical for mills to stand on the same site for generations and we may therefore assume that the 14th-century mill was occupying virtually the same site as the corn mill owned by Lank before the Conquest. The mill standing here in the mid-17th century was known as "Micham Mill alias Wickford Mill alias Marrish Mill"[14] and can thereafter be identified with Mitcham Mill and subsequently the 19th-century Grove Mill, much of which still survives, although recently converted into flats. During the tithe commutation survey of 1846 the Grove Mill was recorded as 'tithe free', which can usually be taken as a sign that the property had once been in the possession of the Church. In the case of the Grove Mill its freedom from tithes can be attributed directly to John de Whitford having granted the tithe of the mill to the newly established priory of St Mary at Southwark in the mid-12th century.

By the 14th century much of the de la Mares' extensive estate was probably leased out to tenants like Thomas de Lodelowe, who died in around 1314 holding 32 acres and 5shillings rent of assize in Mitcham by the service of one-twentieth of a knight's fee. Following his death the land seems to have passed to de Lodelowe's son and heir Thomas, then aged 14.[15]

The circumstances of the deaths of Thomas de Lodelowe senior and John de la Mare, his landlord are not recorded, but the *Victoria County History* comments that "Peter de Montfort only became lord of Ashtead in 1314 on the death of his elder brother, 24 June, at Bannockburn".[16] As one of de Montfort senior's liege men, as well as being related by marriage,[17] John de la Mare would have been expected to follow de Montfort into battle, and it seems highly likely that his tenant Thomas de Lodelowe accompanied them. Certainly men of de Montfort and de la Mare's status would have been mounted, and probably all three were amongst the glittering array of between 2,000 and 3,000 heavily armoured cavalry forming the striking force of Edward II's army. The vain attempt to relieve Stirling Castle before St John's Day 1314 ended in the massacre in the bogs of the Bannock burn – a defeat of the English which is still remembered by the Scots. The deaths of de Montfort, de la Mare and his man de Lodelowe in that year seem more than mere coincidence, and probably all three were slain at the hands of the jubilant clansmen, led to victory by Robert the Bruce.

Florence, who as we have seen was heiress to the estate, was soon involved, together with her husband Philip de Orreby, in a series of land transactions. In 1317, during a cycle of wet summers and failed harvests, she and Philip acquired certain unspecified parcels of land,[18] which were added to the estate, and then, in 1321, Florence and Philip conveyed, presumably by lease, or possibly security for a loan, "two parts of a messuage, a mill, a carucate [about 120 acres of arable] 55 acres of land, 30 of meadow, 10 of pasture and 100s in rent in Mitcham and Morden to William de Herle for life".[19] Florence and Philip may have had a daughter named after her mother (the alternative explanation, offered by the *Victoria County History*, is that Florence had been widowed and remarried) for in 1328 "a settlement was made on Nicholas le Fraunceys and his wife Florence of 9 messuages, 3 tofts, 2 carucates and 56 acres of land, 46 acres of meadow and 60 shillings rent which William de Herle held for life".[20] This would, one imagines, have been intended to secure for Nicholas and Florence an income from the property, but in 1338 they decided to relinquish by quit claim all rights in these lands to de Herle.[21] Lordship of the manor also passed to de Herle at the same time. The reasons for the disposal of these assets are not recorded, and one can only speculate. It is, however, worth noting that by the early part of the century it was becoming increasingly common for landlords, both ecclesiastical and lay, to grant leases of their manors.

In 1347 William de Herle, who had now acquired control of what must have comprised a sizeable portion of the de Mara estate, conveyed the manor to Henry de Strete, a vintner and *nouveau riche* citizen of London. It was intended that lordship would be held by de Strete for life, passing to Thomas de Strete of London, son of Katherine of the Temple.[22] Two years later, when the Black Death had ravaged the population and caused a catastrophic slump in land values, we are told that William Mareys "granted lands and tenements in Mitcham, Wickford, Wandsworth and Carshalton for twenty-one years to Henry de Strete,[23] who had previously purchased land of him".[24]

We thus have an interesting example of the fundamental changes that were taking place in rural society as many old land-owning families were obliged by conditions of economic and demographic stress to relinquish their hold on estates which often had been in their possession since the Conquest. By the early 14th century trading links between

London and the merchants of Bordeaux and Bayonne were strong, and wine from Gascony was a major element in commerce. London vintners prospered, and de Strete typifies the growing number of successful city merchants who, having made their fortunes in trade, began to seek the social status which came with the acquisition of land.

These transactions notwithstanding, it is clear that title to the family's substantial ancestral estate in Mitcham did not pass out of de Mara hands. The taxation records of 1332 had shown William 'Mareys'[25] to be one of the wealthiest men in the parish,[26] and when in 1357 he formally witnessed the mortgaging of Henry de Strete's property in Mitcham, he was still one of the principal landowners in the neighbourhood, with interests in a considerable area of land bordering the Wandle in Lower Mitcham.[27] Five years later, at a time when the country was still under severe strain, he conveyed "his capital messuage with houses over, gardens, crofts, meadows, pastures, woods, trees, hedges, hays and ditches as enclosed, together with two water mills and a piece of moor [i.e. marsh] adjoining as enclosed by the water towards Beneytesfeld and all appurtenances in Wykeford" at 200 shillings per annum to Sir Richard Porter, perpetual vicar of Mitcham and Sir John de Scaldewell, perpetual vicar of "Westmorden".[28]

The acreage is not stated, but the property involved was evidently extensive and, under normal conditions, of considerable value. The mills alone would have brought in a useful income, and mention of enclosed land, crofts and gardens, as well as pasture and woodland, conveys the impression of an estate of appreciable worth to whoever had possession.

Richard Porter had been admitted as vicar of Mitcham 26 June 1361, at the presentation of Southwark priory,[29] but the date of John de Scaldewell's appointment to Morden is not known. (The term 'perpetual vicar' referred to one instituted by the bishop and thus secure from arbitrary removal by the monastic patron of the parish.)

The precise purpose and significance of the conveyance in 1362 is not clear, but it could have been a consequence of depopulation and the decline in the labour force caused by recurrences of the plague. On the other hand, we might see Mareys' action simply as an expression of piety typical of his time, motivated by a desire to show favour to the

Church. Malden suggested the grant may have been in trust for Merton priory, which is plausible, for at an *inquisition post mortem* held in 1380 the prior of Merton was stated to be holding the 'manor' of "Wickford".[30] This is the only reference in local records to such a manor, however, and as employed here the term was probably intended merely to signify an estate or fee over which the prior and convent exercised seigneurial jurisdiction, rather than a conventional manor. Part of the land in Whitford known variously as 'The Marsh Fee Lands', or 'Marrish', remained the freehold of Merton priory until 1538, from the 'farm', or lease, of which the priory was receiving £3 1s 8d at the time of the Dissolution.[31] A further substantial portion of the priory's 'Mareshland' lay to the south, in Morden and Carshalton parishes.

Although it is tempting to see the name Mareshland as derived from the surname Mares, its origin could be descriptive, indicating marsh or marginal land – *'terra marisca'*. Such land, often recently reclaimed or 'inned', was commonly rented rather than held in demesne since its cultivation was inherently risky and the yield could not be relied upon.[32] In Mitcham the Marsh Fee Lands were prone to flooding, and seem to have been kept as pasture or managed as watermeadow – enclosures off Willow Lane were known as the 'Horse Meads' – until the mid-18th century, after which they were used as crofting grounds for the bleaching of calicos. Before the surface level was raised by tipping after the extraction of gravel in the 20th century the land was cultivated as watercress beds. Today these Marsh Fee Lands form part of the Willow Lane industrial estate. Only a fragment bordering the Wandle remains undeveloped, and was set aside in 1993 as the Bennetts Hole nature reserve.

Ravensbury – Medieval Real Estate

As it transpired, the fortunes of the de Stretes were not to prosper, for the campaigns of Edward III and the Black Prince in France, culminating in the victory at Poitiers in 1356 and the depredation by bands of English mercenaries – 'free companies' – in 1357-8, devastated the vineyards and towns of northern France and severely disrupted the wine trade. As if this was not enough, whilst Edward marched from Calais to Reims across an already ravaged countryside, the autumn of 1359 was wet and the vineyards of northern France produced nothing of value. Mortgaging their estates to the prior of Merton evidently failed to enable the de Stretes' business to weather the storm. The wine trade with Gascony was also ruined by 1373, following the failure of John of Gaunt to stem the French re-conquest of south-western France, and we are told by Malden that in 1377-8 "James de Strete conveyed the manor to trustees to himself for life and remainder to John Lord Nevill [*sic*] of Raby, kt., and his heirs."[1]

Neville was a member of one of the old aristocratic families of the North, on whom the kings of England relied to act as a bulwark against the Scots. He had been amongst the great army assembled by Edward III at Calais in 1359 for what in the end was the unsuccessful attempt to capture Reims. Although he enjoyed royal favour (he was one of Edward's councillors) Neville was obliged to resign in 1376 after the impeachment by the Commons of Lord Latimer the Chamberlain and others for mismanagement and corruption. Four years after acquiring the lordship of Ravensbury Neville sold the manor to Sir Robert de Plesyngton,[2] Chief Baron of the Exchequer to Richard II. De Plesyngton promptly resold to Sir John Burghersh,[3] a member of another of the great land-owning warrior families surrounding the Plantagenet throne. These transactions were symptomatic of the breakdown of the feudal system which followed the Black Death, and increasingly from now on we see lordships of manors, having lost much of their original significance, passing from one owner to another as readily disposable assets, much as any other items of real estate.

Sir John Burghersh, whose family were lords of the Carshalton manor of Stone Court,[4] held the lordship of the manor of Ravensbury for ten years, leaving it on his death in 1391 to his two daughters, Margaret, aged 15, and Matilda, who was a little over 12 years of age.[5] We are informed rather quaintly by Manning and Bray that Margaret "married herself to John Grenevylle knt. then living".[6] Lordship of the manor was at this time worth £10 p.a, and was held of Sir Baldwin de Freville as of his manor of Ashtead. The land itself was worth 20shillings. As in the past, six pence or a pair of gilt spurs, were rendered annually in token discharge of all feudal services. After Sir John's death Lady Grenville remarried, taking as her second husband John Arundel of Bideford,[7] by whom she had a son, John. In 1424 John Arundel was recorded as holding the manor of Ravensbury, the inheritance of his late wife, with the reversion belonging to their son, then aged three. The "Manor and parcel thereof" comprised 572 acres of arable worth 4pence an acre, 68 acres of meadow worth 12pence, and 48 shillings was received as rent.[8] The manor itself (i.e. the manorial dues) was valued at £17.[9] As an example of the way in which manorial holdings were becoming intermingled, it is interesting to note that although he was lord of the manor of Ravensbury, Sir John was also a customary tenant of the prior and convent of Christchurch, Canterbury, paying 6shillings a year in discharge of his feudal services for a parcel of land in Mitcham called 'Allmannesland', which lay within the priory's manor of Vauxhall or 'Faukeshall'.[10] According to the *Victoria County History*, the manor went ultimately to the family of Burghersh's other daughter, Matilda. She married Thomas Chaucer, son of the poet, it is believed; their daughter Alice married William de la Pole, duke of Suffolk, whose grandson was John de la Pole, earl of Lincoln, amongst whose possessions the manor was included at his death in 1486/7.[11]

When, late in the 17th century, it became necessary to produce a summary of title to the copyhold estate of Colliers Wood, at the centre of which was a substantial house on what appears to have been a moated site, references were found in the Ravensbury court rolls to 'Jenkingranger'. This house, with its attendant farm buildings, could be traced back to 1486/7.[12] The use of the diminutive 'Jenkin' is interesting, and hints that the property may once have been dubbed 'little John's farm'. Whether this John was the future earl of Lincoln or the three-year old John Arundel we cannot say, although both certainly seem candidates worthy of consideration.

John de la Pole, Richard III's nephew and heir, had been president of the Council of the North. A Yorkist, he unwisely gave support to the impostor, Lambert Simnel, and was slain at the battle of Stoke in 1487 challenging Henry VII's right to the throne. As a consequence of his attainder, the manor of Ravensbury was granted to Simon Digby, whose family was of proven loyalty, to hold 'in tail-male'.[13] It subsequently passed to Charles Brandon, duke of Suffolk,[14] a close friend of Sir Nicholas Carew of Beddington, to whom he sold the manor for £800 in 1531.[15] An extract copy of the court roll shows that with this acquisition Sir Nicholas added to his already extensive estates "200 acres of land, 100 acres of meadow, 200 acres of pasture and 20 acres of wood in the two parishes" (i.e. of Mitcham and Morden).[5] Sir Nicholas later fell from Henry VIII's favour, and was executed in 1539. Lordship of the manor of Ravensbury reverted to the Crown as a result of Carew's attainder, and it was granted, with his other estates, to Thomas Lord Darcy of Chiche. Happily, in January 1554, following the accession of Mary I, Sir Francis Carew, Sir Nicholas's son, was 'restored in the blood', and the family estates, including lordship of Ravensbury, were returned to him.[14]

Ravensbury and the Carews

The 'Marrish', or 'Mareslonde', which prior to the Dissolution had been in the tenure of Merton priory (see p13) and included a messuage, two water mills and 30 acres of land, was granted by Henry VIII in 1544 to Robert Wilford, the new lord of Biggin and Tamworth, a manor which incorporated most of the priory's former estate in north and north-east Mitcham.[1] In 1584, when the 30 acres of 'Marrish' was in the tenure of Bartholomew Clerk, the property was the subject of a dispute between Sir Francis Carew and Charles Howard, a most exalted personage, who was Baron Howard of Effingham, Earl of Nottingham and Lord High Admiral at the time of the Armada. Carew, the defendant, maintained that, together with the house and water mills, the land fell within his manor of Ravensbury, whereas Howard asserted that it was within the jurisdiction of the manor of Reigate. The outcome of the dispute seems not to have been recorded[2] but, given what is known of the tenure of the de Mara estate and the manor of Ravensbury in the 13th and 14th centuries, Carew would seem to have had the better case. As late as 1940 a quit rent was demanded of one of the mills above Mitcham bridge by the steward of Reigate manor, but it was contested.

Ownership of the house, mills and land passed to Bartholomew Clerk's step-son, George Smythe who, in 1594/5, added to the holding by purchase from Henry Whitney and his wife Anne (née Wilford) of four acres adjoining a mill in Carshalton and described as parcel of Mareshlande or Marshfee.[3] Three freehold enclosures totalling 30 acres lying on the north-western side of Willow Lane and captioned "The Marsh Fee Lands" are shown on an estate map drawn by James Cranmer in 1717.[4] Land on the southern side of the lane, comprising part of the South Field, remained copyhold of Ravensbury as late as 1825.[5]

Until early last century, the manor of Ravensbury embraced land on both sides of the Wandle, in the parishes of Mitcham and Morden, as it seems to have done since at least the 14th century. Northwards, it stetched towards Mitcham church as far as Church Path, and a fragment,

The Grove Mill above Mitcham Bridge (c.1906)
This mill seems to have occupied the site of one of the 16th-century mills

Ravensbury Park, survives today as public open space, mainly on the north bank of the river. Until the former Carew estate was broken up and sold for housing purposes early in the 20th century it extended as farmland for a considerable distance to the south, and probably included much of the land held by John de la Mare and his daughter Florence in the 14th century. Also on the Morden side of the Wandle, we may imagine, lies the site of the house and demesne farmstead once belonging to John and Petronilla de la Mare.

For a brief period in the late 16th and early 17th centuries a house on the north bank of the Wandle, and therefore within the parish of Mitcham, was occupied by Nicholas, the son of Sir Nicholas Throckmorton and Anne Carew.[6] On being adopted by his childless uncle Sir Francis Carew, who died unmarried in 1611, Nicholas Thockmorton (who was himself knighted in 1603) took the surname of Carew and succeeded to the family estates in Surrey, which included lordship of the manor.[7] His first wife was Mary, daughter of Sir George More of Loseley, and sister-in-law of John Donne, who was resident in Mitcham for a short period in the early years of the 17th century.

Having inherited the family estates Nicholas Throckmorton Carew was a wealthy man, and no doubt made his late uncle's great house at Beddington his home. Francis Carew, his eldest son, is usually described as 'of Ravensbury', but is likely to have used the manor house at Mitcham only rarely. Elected member of Parliament for Haslemere in 1624 and Guildford in 1627, Francis married Susan, daughter of Sir William Romney, and received a knighthood sometime before 1639. He was defeated as the candidate for Bletchingly in the election to the short Parliament of 1640, and seems to have continued to reside at Court. In 1642 he joined King Charles I at Oxford but was not in the army and, although fined heavily by Parliament, had his estates returned to him in 1644. The Carews, however, were to be in financial difficulty throughout the Commonwealth, and eventually their estates were mortgaged.[8]

The records of the manor of Ravensbury survive from around the time of Simon Digby's tenure, and various documents from 1488 until 1642 are in the Manuscript Department of the British Library.[9] Another collection, including, amongst other items, numerous memoranda concerning waste and common land in the manor, notes of admissions to and surrenders of tenancy from the reign of Henry VII to the 17th century, and the court rolls from 1650 to 1921, was transferred to the care of the Surrey Record Office in 1969, and are now in Surrey History Centre.[10] Records from the 18th century onwards are copious and well kept. They include many references to copyhold property in Mitcham as far apart as Willow Lane and Colliers Wood, and are a valuable source for local studies, recording the tenure of copyhold properties and casting light on the more mundane aspects of manorial administration in the 18th and 19th centuries. The histories of Tamworth Farm (opposite Figges Marsh), Eagle House, houses around the Upper Green, Prospect House and The Cedars on Commonside East, plus various dwellings and parcels of land overlooking the Three Kings Pond are thus quite easily traced.

An explanation has already been offered of the inclusion of Colliers Wood in the manor of Ravensbury, and Tamworth Farm may have become part of the manor in the same way. Properties in the vicinity of the Upper Green and the Three Kings Piece held copyhold of Ravensbury in the 19th century are also strangely detached from the rest of the manor, and are unlikely to have been included within the original estate held by Sir William de la Mare in the Middle Ages. The site of Eagle House, and probably that of 'Old Bedlam' (a large house that once overlooked the Upper Green), were at one time the property of Elizabeth Throckmorton, wife of Sir Walter Raleigh, and the best explanation that can be offered is that they, and a number of houses nearby, accrued to the manor as part of the Carews' Mitcham estate. Whether or not their predecessors had originally been subject to feudal tenure one cannot say, but copyholders in the 18th and 19th centuries were required to pay annual quit rents, and were charged a substantial fee by the Carew estate if they wished to enter into a deed of enfranchisement to convert their property to freehold.

The End of the Manor

Through various vicissitudes lordship of the manor of Ravensbury and ownership of various properties in Mitcham were to remain in the hands

In Chancery.

Between WALTER HENRY HAYWARD, ... Plaintiff,
and
Cranmer HARrison HAYWARD COOKS and others, Defendants
And Between WALTER HENRY HAYWARD, ... Plaintiff,
and
JAMES EDWARD CHAPMAN and another, ... Defendants.

By order of Trustees.

PARTICULARS AND CONDITIONS OF SALE

OF

The Ravensbury Estate,

SITUATE

IN THE PARISHES OF MITCHAM AND MORDEN.

IN THE COUNTY OF SURREY.

A

FREEHOLD PROPERTY,

(PART LAND TAX REDEEMED)

Containing altogether upwards of

THREE HUNDRED ACRES,

THE MANOR HOUSE,

WITH LAWNS, SHRUBBERIES, GARDENS & LAKES,

(The latter affording TROUT FISHING)

Coach houses, Stabling, &c., with Meadow Land situated, containing 12a. 3a. 9r.; late in the occupation of John Gayfere, Esq. (but now unoccupied)

ALSO

The PARK AND LANDS ATTACHED,

Immediately in front of the above described Estate, and only separated from it by the River (offering
Desirable Frontages) with sites calculated for the erection of a Mansion, or Houses, possessing fine Views, and
situated close to the Brighton Turnpike Road from Sutton to London, containing 120a. 1r. 36r., with neat
FARM COTTAGE, LABOURERS COTTAGE, & AGRICULTURAL BUILDING,
in the occupation of Mr. Charles Prior.

ALSO

A FREEHOLD FARM,

Containing 98a. 3r. 10r. with suitable COTTAGES & AGRICULTURAL BUILDINGS, held by Henry J.
Hart, Esq.

A VILLA RESIDENCE.

With LAWN, SHRUBBERY, GARDENS, ORCHARD & PADDOCK, together &c. On. Str., with Yards, Coach-house, Stabling, &c., let to The Rev. Rvd. Taunton.

THE SNUFF AND TOBACCO MILLS,

With DWELLING HOUSE, Gardens, &c., let to Messrs. Butter.

SHAWL & LINEN PRINTING MANUFACTORY & PREMISES,

With Dwelling House, Gardens, and Meadows attached, containing 14. 0a. &c.

LITTLE GRASS FARM,

With COTTAGE, GARDEN, & BUILDINGS Place & Pasture, containing &c. let also to Mr. James Lamb.

FOUR PARCELS OF MOST VALUABLE ARABLE LAND,

Used as PHYSIC GARDEN, containing &c. let also to Mr. Potts.

A MEADOW,

Adjoining the Railroad to Merstham containing 14. 0a. 12p. adapted for building upon, this lately occupied by Mr. Gifford, but now to Let.

SIX FREEHOLD COTTAGES, WITH GARDENS,

In Morden Lane, held by Mrs. Nun, and others.

SEVERAL PARCELS OF MARKET GARDEN & PHYSIC GROUND.

Containing together 14. &c. &c., in the respective occupation of Messrs. Biggs, Pinkins, Simmons, and others.

The Estate is within a quarter of an hours drive of the Wimbledon Station, by a new turnpike from Croydon, and

THE ABOVE PROPERTY WILL BE SOLD BY AUCTION,

BY

MR. JOSEPH NASH,

(Of the Firm of Messrs. JOSEPH & JOHN NASH, of Reigate, the Auctioneers appointed by the Judge to sell the same)

AT THE AUCTION MART, LONDON

On FRIDAY, the 20th day of JULY, 1855, at Twelve for One o'clock;

IN EIGHT LOTS.

The first page of the Sales Particulars of 1855, reproduced by courtesy of Surrey History Service

of the Carew family for some 350 years. The quarter sessions records show Sir Nicholas Carew acting as a leading justice for the division of the county covering Beddington, Carshalton, Croydon and Mitcham for much of the early 17th century, and for many years the family held a distinguished position in local society. The break-up of the Carew estates commenced after the succession of young Charles Hallowell Hallowell Carew to the property on the death of his father, Captain Charles Hallowell Carew, in 1849. Already heavily in debt to moneylenders, 'Charlie' Carew gambled all on a horse and lost. Proceedings for bankruptcy were instituted in 1857, and an Act of Parliament was necessary "to execute the disentailing of the estate and its mortgages, and to settle a legal wrangle".[1]

Lordship of the manor remained with the Carews for another half century nevertheless, and manorial rights continued to be exercised. They were still a source of income, as is evidenced by a deed of enfranchisement granted in September 1890 by Frank Murrey Maxwell Hallowell Carew to Emma Jane Bartley, owner of Chestnut Cottage, which overlooks the Cricket Green, or 'Wickford Green', as it was referred to in the court rolls. The indenture describes Miss Bartley as "one of the copyholders or customary tenants" of the manor, holding the property "at the will of the lord". For the sum of £90 paid to Carew's steward she was released from observance of the customs of the manor and the liability to meet the fines, heriots, quit rents, suits and services demanded of the customary tenantry. The rights over Mitcham Common and, in particular, the right "to the opening and working of gravel pits thereon" (a potentially valuable asset) were retained by the lord of the manor.[2]

In 1907 the remaining manorial rights of Ravensbury were sold by Frank Carew to the Prince's Golf Club, but with the newly created Board of Conservators of Mitcham Common being given the option to purchase at the original price after a certain period of years.[3] By this time there were only a few copyholds unenfranchised, and the main incentive to purchase was to strengthen further the Conservators' powers designed to save the Common from destruction at the hands of those wishing to dig sand and gravel, and to preserve its natural features. The manor effectively came to an end in 1926 when, by Act of Parliament, copyhold tenure was abolished.

RAVENSBURY MANOR HOUSE

The Ruins

On the north bank of the Wandle in Ravensbury Park, partially hidden from view by a thick growth of trees and shrubs, three fragments of neatly pointed yellow brick walling can be found, all that remains visible above ground of Ravensbury Manor House.[1] Until the 1970s the ruins were effectively protected from the attention of marauding children by a rectangle of substantial chain-link fencing, but this barrier became increasingly dilapidated, and the failure of the Parks Department of the London Borough of Merton to effect satisfactory repairs resulted in the remaining brickwork becoming vandalised. In 1994, in an effort to salvage the situation and funded by a grant from the Council's Conservation Areas Advisory Committee, the brickwork was stabilised and consolidated in lime mortar by contractors working under the direction of the Leisure Services Department. Regrettably the Parks Department considered reinstatement of the fencing low in their priorities, and still did nothing to protect the wall. By the end of the year

Ravensbury Manor House from the Sales Particulars of 1855
reproduced by courtesy of Surrey History Service

the rebedded bricks had been largely dislodged, and the destruction of what survived of the original walling was continuing.

The ruins are, in fact, from the last phase of the house, when a stylish late 18th-century wing was added to the riverside elevation of a far older building of which no visible trace survives. Known simply as Ravensbury House, the property was last occupied in the mid-19th century, but its precise fate thereafter seems not to have been recorded. Many years later "old Ravensbury Manor House" was remembered by one old resident of Mitcham as a "striking landmark" to be seen from the river in the 1880s, but was said to have fallen into decay and is believed to have been largely demolished in about 1882.[2] Parts were obviously left standing, however, probably to lend an air of mystery and romance to what had then become part of the grounds surrounding the house called 'Ravensbury Park' erected in 1864 on a site off Bishopsford Road.

Early Years – The Carews and the Garths

Very little is known of the early history of the site, the original house or, indeed, the role it or its successors played in the history of the manor. The ruins have engendered mild curiosity ever since the park was opened to the public in 1929, and their antiquarian interest was not ignored by the cartographers of the Ordnance Survey, for in the inter-war years the site was customarily marked on the maps as 'Manor House', in the Gothic script reserved for antiquities. When a small exploratory excavation was conducted near the site of the house by the writer and other members of Merton Historical Society in 1973 a few sherds of typical coarse pottery of the 13th and 14th centuries were found, indicative of occupation in the vicinity during the Middle Ages, but little of significance was added to what had already been suspected.[3] At one time a house nearby may have been a residence of the lord of the manor, but the documentary evidence surviving from the 17th century seems to indicate that it was not a particularly large building, and more suited to occupation by a junior member of the family, or the manor steward. As we have seen in the previous chapter, throughout the Middle Ages there are references to houses and 'messuages' owned by the de

Mara or de la Mare family, one of which, quite possibly, occupied a site by the waterside at Ravensbury. Old Ravensbury Lane, leading from Mitcham to Morden, passed close by and, until recently, on the opposite bank of the river stood 'Ravensbury Farm'. This building, however, was barely a century old, and was on the site chosen in the mid-18th century by John Arbuthnot of Ravensbury Manor House for a new farmstead, all trace of which has now gone. It remains a reasonable assumption that a manor house stood nearby in the 13th century, and that archaeological work in the future will demonstrate not only its site, but that its origins predated the Conquest.

The picture begins to clear during the reign of Elizabeth I, and between 1569 and 1579 there are several documentary references to lands bordering the Wandle in Mitcham owned by Sir Francis Carew of Beddington and leased to Richard Hopkin, his 'fermor' or tenant. One such document, of 1572, mentions the "oulde orchard of one Rasberie"[4] and "long poole Lane", which might, conceivably, be a reference to Ravensbury Lane, now reduced to a cul-de-sac leading to a service gate into Ravensbury Park, beyond which the old way is followed by an arcade of mature plane trees surrounding a path leading to the riverside. It is believed that towards the close of the 16th century Ravensbury House, or its predecessor, was occupied by Nicholas, son of Sir Nicholas Throckmorton and Anne Carew.[5] As we have seen, in 1611 Nicholas took the surname Carew and succeeded to the family estates, which included a substantial part of Lower Mitcham. He was knighted in 1603 and, on being widowed, he had remarried in 1616.[6]

During the reign of James I the manor house of Ravensbury became the residence of Alexander Garth, styled "of Ravensbury" in the bishop's visitation of Surrey in 1623. A younger son of Richard Garth, lord of the manor of Morden, and his second wife, Joan Wells, Alexander had married Alice Ward or Worde, daughter of the rector of Beddington, on 29 May 1609,[7] and the Mitcham parish register records the baptisms of nine Garth children, four boys and five girls, between 1613 and 1626.

The Mitcham hearth tax assessments of 1664 include a house belonging to Sir Nicholas Carew, which then had six hearths, and clearly was only of modest size. No other property in Mitcham is listed on which Carew was taxed, and there seems no reason to believe the house was other than at Ravensbury. The occupier at this time was a lady by the name of Elizabeth Watts, about whom we have no other information, other than her succeeding her husband in the tenancy.[8]

A rent roll of the manor, undated but ascribed to the latter part of the 17th century, describes the "Mansion howse called Ravensbury", with its "One Dovehouse, One great Barne, a Storehouse, a Stable, Two gardens, two Orchards" and some 90 acres of land in Mitcham, as being in the tenure of "Henry Hampson Esq".[9] A member of the Merchant Taylors' Company since 1663, Hampson was also a member of the East India Company, and is known to have had an address in Bull and Mouth Street, Aldersgate, in 1677.[10] His parents had been resident in Mitcham since the early 1650s, occupying a large house in Lower Mitcham later to become known as Mitcham Hall, but had moved away by 1668. The father died in 1677, shortly after which, having probably inherited part of the family estate, Henry Hampson took up residence in the parish. He died in March 1691, and lies interred in a vault beneath the floor of the north aisle of Mitcham parish church, where a black marble ledger stone to his memory could be seen, until a new raised floor was installed in 1991.[11]

Occupancy of the house at Ravensbury after Henry Hampson's death has not been traced, but could possibly be ascertained from the rent rolls. It is tempting to wonder whether another generation of Garths may have made their home here, for Richard, son of Richard Garth IV of Morden, was baptised at Mitcham in June 1724, and Boevey, his brother, in June 1725. The younger Richard was responsible for the building of the present Morden Hall around 1750, but the family's previous home in the area has not been identified. Other branches of the family had maintained links with Mitcham over the years, for a Richard Garth was buried in Mitcham church in 1664, and George in 1673. When in 1686 a Mrs Anne Garth died in London, it was to Mitcham that she was brought for burial. The death of Richard Garth III is recorded in the Mitcham parish register, although it is noted that in his case the burial took place at Morden.[12]

The Arbuthnots of Ravensbury

Mitcham vestry minutes show that in about 1753[13] John Arbuthnott (sic), described as the proprietor of "a most extensive manufactory" at Ravensbury, was living at 'Ravensbury House'. Two years later, by a lease dated November 1755, Sir Nicholas Hackett Carew granted land and appurtenances in Mitcham and "Moredon", including Ravensbury Manor House, to Arbuthnot for 99 years. This was confirmed by an indenture dated September 1764, between Arbuthnot and Carew's trustee, William Pellat of Croydon (Carew having died in 1762), assigning "all that capital messuage called 'Ravensbury Manor House' with the barns, outhouses and buildings thereunto belonging," together with "Fields arable and pasture in Mitcham and Morden".[14]

Arbuthnot was involved in calico printing, an industry which, from the early 18th century until the middle of the Victorian period, flourished in the Wandle valley. Arbuthnot had been in partnership with John Cecil of Merton Abbey, whose daughter, Sally Margaret, he married in 1753, and was also related by marriage to the Mauvillains, a wealthy and successful Huguenot family, who had established a printing works at Ravensbury on land immediately downstream from the manor house in about 1700. Fortunes were to be made at this time from the printing of the enormously popular chintzes and calicoes, and the Ravensbury works continued in production, albeit in different hands and with declining profitability, until the 1860s. The full history of printing at Ravensbury is dealt with in a following chapter.

The Mitcham poor rate books make it clear from a doubling of the rateable value that soon after negotiating the lease of the Ravensbury property Arbuthnot set about enlarging the house very considerably. At the same time (1753) he obtained the consent of Mitcham vestry to the diversion of the road to Morden, which passed close by his residence, and to the removal of the old bridge which crossed the river at this point. In this he had the support of his landlord, Sir Nicholas Hacket Carew[14] Obviously the diversion was aimed at securing greater privacy for the house, and for his part Arbuthnot accepted liability for the repair of the new bridge and road he had constructed past Ravensbury mill, a few hundred yards downstream. The vestry minutes acknowledge that he had faithfully discharged this liability.

Sixty years later, over the question of responsibility for repair of the new bridge, which had fallen into decay, the vestry found itself in dispute with Colonel Hugh Arbuthnot, a distant relative who had inherited tenure of the estate. The vestry sought counsel's opinion, asking if they had any power to enforce the repair of the bridge by Arbuthnot and, if not, whether they would be entitled to "open the ancient Highway leading close by Ravensbury House", which would "ruin it as a Gentleman's Residence which it is now." If neither course were open to them, the vestry asked if the parish was liable for the cost of the repair of the new bridge. In giving his opinion William Draper Best of Norwood, their counsel, held that as the landowner, that is, Carew, had not been a party to the original agreement, the old road had not been closed formally. It could therefore be repaired and reinstated as a common way, and either the old or new bridge should be repaired by the county.

On hearing this decision the vestry, through their solicitor, informed the colonel that they hoped the controversy could be settled without the vestry having to open the old road, and that he would repair the new one. The question of works to the bridge was not raised again, and the matter was presumably left to the county. The final outcome is not recorded in the vestry minutes, from which one may conclude that the dispute was settled without further recourse to law. As we have seen, part of the old road survives to the present day, but is no longer a public highway, whilst the Morden Road continues to make a detour around what were formerly the Ravensbury bleaching grounds before crossing the Wandle by the bridge adjoining Ravensbury mills.

John Arbuthnot's seal is heraldic, and he seems to have been related through a cadet branch to the great Scottish family of the same name. Sally Arbuthnot née Cecil died in February 1759, and her father a year later. Both were buried at Morden.[15] John remained the ratepayer at Ravensbury until about 1780, having remarried in 1761, his second wife being Ursula Fitzgerald of Taplow. In 1762 Arbuthnot married again (Ursula having died the previous year), his third wife being Anne Stone, daughter of Richard Stone, a London banker, whose seat was Rockfleet Castle, Co. Mayo.[16] In the late 18th century large quantities of Irish linen were being imported into England for finishing, and there is record of Arbuthnot holding office under the Irish Linen Board.

We know that John Arbuthnot was resident in Mitcham in 1763 and 1764, for in March each year his name was put forward to the justices for selection as surveyor of highways for the parish during the ensuing years. He also signed the vestry minutes in March 1765. There are, furthermore, the baptisms of seven Arbuthnot children, three boys and four girls, recorded in the Mitcham registers betwen 1764 and 1773. Three Arbuthnots find a place in the *Dictionary of National Biography*: The Right Honourable Charles Arbuthnot, born in 1767, became a close friend of the Duke of Wellington after a career as a diplomat and politician, and his brothers Robert and Thomas both received knighthoods and attained the rank of lieutenant-general during the course of distinguished careers in the army.[17] A Charles Arbuthnot, son of John Arbuthnot of Ravensbury, was baptised privately at Mitcham in April 1767, but there is no record of Robert or Thomas. Robert was born in 1773, and it is therefore quite possible that he was baptised in Ireland.

Like many of his contemporaries John Arbuthnot's interests were very much wider than the production and embellishment of textiles.[18] The 'agrarian revolution' of the late 18th century was led by innovators like Coke of Norfolk and 'Turnip' Townsend, who introduced new methods of farming, including the marling of soils to improve fertility and the growing of root crops as fodder, thus facilitating the over-wintering of livestock. Another was Robert Bakewell of Leicester, whose selective breeding of cattle and sheep greatly improved English blood lines. New ideas such as these were taken up with enthusiasm all over the country.

In a letter to Edmund Burke in June 1774 the Marquis of Rockingham, who rented a house at Wimbledon between 1771 and 1782 and was actively applying the new practices on farms on his estates, observed that "I have passed a pleasant day at Duckets Farm with some gentlemen farmers who afterwards dined there. Arbuthnot met us and dined here – he seems so right in his ideas." Duckets Farm, I understand from Dr Veale, was at Petersham. According to Sutherland "John Arbuthnot of Mitcham" was "notice as a farmer *c.*1760", and Mingay comments that with Duckett, Arbuthnot was one of the "two leading experimental farmers whose names are coupled with that of Bakewell".[18] In November 1768 Arbuthnot leased from Richard Garth a farm in Lower Morden, later known as Peacock Farm (the Victorian house of which is now part of Wyevale garden centre). The reorganisation of the Garth holdings in Lower Morden, from small farmsteads with lands in scattered closes into four large and fairly compact farms, dates from this period, perhaps under Arbuthnot's influence.[19]Arbuthnot's contribution to farming was long remembered, and in June 1811 Arthur Young delivered a lecture On *the Husbandry of three celebrated British farmers, Messrs. Bakewell. Arbuthnot and Ducket* to the Board of Agriculture.

From the middle of the 18th century local administration became more efficient, if we may judge from the records that survive. Books containing the assessments for the poor rate and later the land tax are preserved at Surrey History Centre, and form an unbroken series from 1770 until 1831. Despite the absence of addresses, it is a relatively easy matter for the researcher to trace the larger houses, whose higher assessments make them conspicuous in the records. From John Arbuthnot's time onwards the history of Ravensbury House and that of the print works diverge, the one continuing for nearly a century as a private house, whilst the other, in separate occupation, remained a centre of industry.

The head lease of the Ravensbury estate stayed in the Arbuthnot family's hands for many years, and in 1779, when John Arbuthnot's business affairs had placed him in financial difficulties and he was living in France, Ravensbury House became the seat of Admiral Marriott Arbuthnot.[20] This was during a short spell of service in England when Arbuthnot, having been advanced to flag rank, was recalled in 1778 from Halifax, Nova Scotia, where he had been commissioner of the navy since 1775. In the spring of 1779 Arbuthnot sat as a member of Admiral Keppel's court marshall, but his residence at Ravensbury was brief, for on 1 May 1779, having been appointed to the command of the North American station, he left England on the 64-gun *Europe*.

A contemporary writer, compiling a traveller's guide in about 1789, described Ravensbury House as lying about three furlongs from the Morden Road, in a pleasant rural situation, upon the north banks of the Wandle. "The walks, which extend a considerable distance on the river side, are bounded with handsome shrubberies", he informed his readers, "which, with the large lawn on the south belonging to the 'Grove' [a long curving stretch of grassland which was a feature of the Ravensbury estate and is now partly preserved at Moreton Green] add much to the beauty of the place."[21] Ravensbury was clearly a most desirable haven for retirement, but for Marriot Arbuthnot its attractions were to be enjoyed only briefly. As far as one can judge from local records, the admiral played little part in the affairs of the parish of Mitcham, but had the intention existed, the opportunities were few.

Described by his detractors as "a coarse, blustering, foul-mouthed bully", "ignorant of the discipline of his profession" and "destitute of even a rudimentary knowledge of naval tactics", Marriot Arbuthnot's nevertheless remarkable career is outlined in the *Dictionary of National Biography*.[22] He was born in about 1711, a native of Weymouth, but very little is known of his parentage and early life. Joining the Royal Navy as a boy, he attained the rank of lieutenant in 1739, became a commander in 1746 and captain in 1747. In 1759 he commanded the *Portland* in the blockade of Quiberon Bay, and a guardship at Portsmouth from 1771 to 1773. His three year's posting at Halifax was probably well suited to a man of his age and service, but Arbuthnot was not destined for a peaceful retirement. Elevation to flag rank and the new command was no sinecure, and he is said to have held a blustering but querulous, active but ineffective, command of the squadron in American waters until relieved of his duties at his own request in 1781. His achievements were not insignificant, however, and the assessment seems unduly harsh, for Arbuthnot was approaching 70 years of age when called back to active service.

Having acting in concert with General Sir Henry Clinton in the successful expedition to Charlestown, Arbuthnot repositioned his squadron at the approaches to Long Island, then in enemy hands, to ward off reinforcement by the French fleet. Here he remained throughout the summer of 1780 until he was unexpectedly superseded by Sir George Rodney in a move he strongly resented, and on which he expressed his feelings with much ill-temper and insolence. The Admiralty supported Rodney, however, and Arbuthnot, thoroughly annoyed at the implied censure, applied to be relieved of his command, pleading ill-health. Clinton and Rodney, with whom Arbuthnot remained at constant odds, both threatened to resign unless he was promptly withdrawn, the general, it is said, being kept in terror of losing supremacy at sea due to Arbuthnot constantly changing his plans. In the event, the admiral was not recalled, and neither Clinton nor Rodney resigned. In the summer of 1781, after a furious engagement with the French fleet under Destouches, during which both squadrons suffered considerable damage, Arbuthnot's request for permission to return to England was granted, and he surrendered his command to Rear-Admiral Graves. On returning home he seems not to have reoccupied Ravensbury House, but took a year's lease of the nearby Growtes.[23] Thereafter he appears to have moved away from the district, although he evidently maintained connections with Mitcham, for in February 1789 he was appointed to the committee of gentlemen charged with the task of raising funds for the renovation of the parish church. Arbuthnot saw no further service at sea, but by seniority was appointed Admiral of the Blue Squadron in 1793, and was given the command of the *Cerberus*, then being built at Buckler's Hard, in Hampshire.[24] Early the following year, on 31 January, the old sea dog died in London at the age of 83.[22]

'Ravensbury House' – undated watercolour by William Wood Fenning (1799-1872), whose grandfather and father were proprietors of the printworks, possibly during an 1850 visit, reproduced by courtesy of Sue Wilmott

The Last Years of the Old Manor House: 1800–*c*.1860

For the six years following Admiral Arbuthnot's death the old manor house seems to have lacked a tenant and then, in 1800, after considerable improvements and extensions had been carried out – these are reflected in the increased land tax assessments – the house was occupied by Chamberlain Goodwin. His tenure of Ravensbury House was of short duration, however, and in 1803 a sub-lease was granted by Colonel Hugh Arbuthnot to Mrs Frances Barnard.[25] Frances Barnard was the widow of William Barnard (1735-1795), a third-generation member of a dynasty of shipbuilders at Deptford which built extensively both for the Navy Board and the Honourable East India Company. William Barnard was one of the most successful and respected builders on the Lower Thames, at that time the centre of mercantile shipbuilding in the United Kingdom. Frances retained an interest in her late husband's business until her death in 1825.[26] She was buried at Deptford, where she and her late husband had been members of the Butt Lane (High Street) Congregational Church.[27]

Frances Barnard's landlord, the Hon. Sir Hugh Arbuthnot, KCB, of Hatton-Bervie, the second son of the 7th Viscount Arbuthnot, joined the 49th Regiment of Foot as an ensign in 1796. He served with the rank of captain in the campaign in Holland in 1799, including the battle of Egmont-op-Zee, and also aboard the *Ganges* at the battle of Copenhagen in 1801, for which he was awarded a naval medal. With the rank of major he served for a short period with the 14th Garrison Battalion, and was then transferred to the 52nd Foot, which he commanded at the bombardment of Copenhagen and the action at Kioge in 1807. He served in the expedition to Sweden under Sir John Moore in 1808, and in Portugal and Spain, being present in the retreat from Sahagun and at the battle of Corunna, where Sir John was killed. With the Light Division Arbuthnot saw action on the Coa, and he commanded the 52nd Foot in the Lines of Torres Vedras and the battle of Busaco. He was also present at the battle of Fuentes d'Onor. For his service at Busaco he received a gold medal, and a silver medal with clasps for Corunna and Fuentes d'Onor. The army remained Arbuthnot's profession for the whole of his life. He became a brevet lieutenant-colonel in 1811, colonel of the 38th Foot in 1843, and general in 1854. In 1826 he entered politics, becoming member of parliament for Kincardineshire, a constituency which he represented in ten parliaments until 1865. The 79th Regiment of Foot (later the Cameron Highlanders) accorded him his final honour in 1862 by appointing him colonel of the regiment, a position he was to hold until his death in 1868.[28]

Throughout the reign of George IV Ravensbury House continued to attract the attention of topographical writers and artists, a guide book to Surrey published in 1823, for instance, describing it as "an extensive ancient mansion with pleasure-grounds and plantations also of great extent".[29] James Bourne had been inspired to sketch the house from the river some 20 years previously,[30] and Yates painted it in 1825, choosing the picturesque rear for a charming watercolour which can be seen in Merton Local Studies Centre.[31] From this viewpoint the house might well have dated from the late 17th or early 18th century, with sliding sash windows under a red-tiled roof. An overhanging top storey supported on a colonnade could indicate an earlier timber-framed house behind a later façade. The yellow stock brick southern elevation, of two

'Mitcham – Ravensbury Manor House – Mrs Barnard'
A rear view in a watercolour by Yates, dated 1825, in Extra-Illustrated
copy of E W Brayley's History of Surrey *(Vol.III)*
reproduced by courtesy of Merton Library & Heritage Service

storeys and five bays terminating in a parapet above which the tiled roof was barely visible, is shown in another sketch by an as yet unidentified artist.[27] This façade is clearly later than the rest of the house, and may be part of the alterations carried out for Chamberlain Goodwin around 1800. It is from the two corner pilasters and the central bowed entrance porch of the south front that the remaining fragments derive.

Ravensbury House was retained for a few years by Frances Barnard's executors, but in 1827 the adjoining land in Morden, that she had held with the house, was leased for 21 years to Henry Hoare of the neighbouring Mitcham Grove.[32] He died in 1828, and by 1831 the remaining portion of the lease seems to have passed into the hands of Sir John Lubbock, the banker, who is listed as the occupier of the house and lands in the land tax records. Sir John did not actually live in the house, for in 1828 he had purchased from Henry Hoare's executors the far larger Mitcham Grove, the grounds of which adjoined those of Ravensbury. For the next 16 years the history of the house is a blank, apart from its being used by the girls from the Mitcham National Schools whilst some necessary repairs were carried out to the school building overlooking the Lower Green West.

The census returns of 1841 have no recognisable entry for Ravensbury House, which would suggest it was then unoccupied, but by 1846, when the tithe survey was conducted, the property had become a private residence once more. The new occupant, John Gifford, was described in the census of 1851 as a 'Colonial Broker'. His landlord was Captain Charles Hallowell Carew. Then aged 63, Gifford had probably retired from active business life and with his wife was enjoying the peace and beauty of his riverside retreat. If he was an angler, he would have not lacked for sport, for the Wandle and its backwaters were at this time highly regarded, both for the size and number of their trout. The estate embraced 15 acres of garden and meadow lying between the Wandle and Morden Road, beyond which unspoilt countryside stretched away towards Sutton. The entrance drive from Morden Road was the 'ancient highway' diverted by John Arbuthnot, separated and screened from the Ravensbury printworks, once one had passed the park gates, by a shrubbery, an artificial waterway and a long brick wall. Five servants were living in when the census was conducted, and other staff lived in a group of cottages which, with hothouses and kitchen gardens, occupied a site close to Morden Road.

Some years ago, near the site of these cottages, a length of elm water pipe was discovered during the course of work on the nearby backwater of the Wandle.[33] Whether the pipe had anything to do with the cottages or the printworks, it is difficult to say, but in view of the very considerable use made of the river water in bleaching and dyeing, the latter possibility is the more likely. As late as 1932, when the Ordnance Survey conducted a revisionary survey, the evidence for parallel ditches, probably serving old bleaching grounds, survived in what had then become a public park. Today, when the sun is low, they can still be detected as depressions running across the open area in the centre. In Gifford's time, as Braithwaite observed in 1853, the stream flowing through the grounds was purely ornamental, and its trout were "very abundant".[34]

During the 1850s George Parker Bidder, who was then resident at Mitcham House (later known as Mitcham Hall), was engaged in the process of purchasing an estate which eventually embraced 180 acres on both sides of the Wandle below Mitcham bridge as far as the Ravensbury snuff mills. The enforced sale of the Carew estate in 1855 offered the opportunity for him to purchase Ravensbury House and its grounds, but the print works, lying between Ravensbury Lane, Morden Road and the river, were not acquired by Bidder and the land passed eventually into the hands of Gilliat Hatfeild of Morden Hall.[35]

The Giffords were followed at Ravensbury House by a Mr Hitchcock, who also held the property on a lease. He was soon in dispute with the firm of Dempsey and Heard, whose shawl printing at the adjacent works resulted in the discharge of quantities of chemicals into the Wandle.[36] The pollution ceased with the collapse of the firm in the early 1860s. As far as we can tell, Hitchcock and his family were the last residents at Ravensbury, and the house must have fallen into decay soon after their departure, although the precise date is uncertain. Robert Masters Chart, born in 1850, could recall seeing the old house, or its ruins, remembering it as "an impressive landmark on the bank of the river.[37] It is shown in outline only on the 25-inch Ordnance Survey map of 1865/6, which suggests that it was already empty and derelict by the time the survey was in progress.

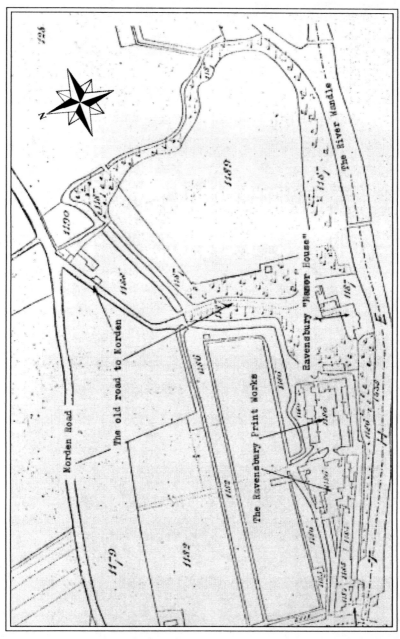

Annotated detail from the Mitcham Tithe Map of 1846 (70% reduction) reproduced by courtesy of Surrey History Service

Ravensbury and the Bidders[38]

George Parker Bidder was born in Devon in 1806, the son of a
Moretonhampstead building contractor and stonemason. He soon
demonstrated an extraordinary ability for mental calculations and, such
were his talents and the ease with which he could provide answers to
the most complex mathematical problems, his father found it profitable
to tour the country with the boy, exhibiting him as "a calculating
phenomenon" before royalty and parties of the nobility and gentry.
Fortunately young George's talent attracted the attention of certain
eminent men who secured him an education, first briefly at Wilson's
school, Camberwell, and later at Edinburgh University. He did not
proceed to a degree (many students in those days did not consider it
worth while, and relied on certificates of attendance as the necessary
verification of having studied their subjects) and in 1825 Bidder secured
a junior post in the Ordnance Survey. The following year he was recruited
as a surveyor by the civil engineer H R Palmer, an associate of Telford
and a prime mover in the foundation of the Institution of Civil Engineers
– of which many years later George Bidder was to become President.

Bidder had the good fortune to have reached maturity during the great
period of Victorian civil engineering, and formed a close association
with Robert Stephenson, who became a personal friend and a frequent
visitor to Mitcham. Bidder's appointment as a member of the engineering
staff on the London and Birmingham Railway in 1834 was the first step
in a career which took him to many parts of the World, and included
involvement in what became the Great Eastern Railway, and also
railways in Denmark and Norway, and the Scinde, Punjab and Delhi
railway in India. The construction of the Victoria Docks was perhaps
his greatest work, but much nearer to home he is still remembered for
his association with Morton Peto in the Wimbledon and Croydon Joint
Railway Company and the link line through Mitcham (one of many
being built or planned in South London) which opened in 1855.[39]

As we have seen, within a few years of having settled in Mitcham
George Parker Bidder commenced purchasing land in Mitcham and
Morden which was to be transformed into a new park. He was aided in
this by the break-up of the Carew estates, and the auction of the

Ravensbury Estate in 1855, in accordance with a decree of the High Court of Chancery, provided the opportunity to purchase the then empty Ravensbury Manor House and its adjacent gardens and parkland lying in Mitcham and Morden. Ravensbury, or Morden, Farm and 93 acres of meadow and arable land on the south bank of the Wandle were offered at the same sale, but were purchased by the sitting tenant, Henry James Hoare, owner of the adjoining property, The Lodge. Around 1860 Bidder bought farmland opposite his own lying on the south-eastern side of Bishopsford Road. Part of this land – the so-called 'Hilly Fields' – he gave to his brother, Samuel Parker Bidder, who had recently returned from Canada, as the site for the new house he wished to build. By 1863, with 'Hill Field' as it was known, ready for occupation, Samuel Bidder was completing the finishing touches by laying out the gardens. The house has now disappeared, but the name is perpetuated in Hillfield Avenue, a cul-de-sac estate of houses erected in the early 1930s.

In the summer of 1864, the sale of the freehold of Mitcham Hall to Sydney Gedge having been agreed, George Parker Bidder moved his household to 'Ravensbury Park', a new house built for him off the Sutton road, close to the point where Seddon Road now joins Bishopsford Road. The extensive grounds of the house – the newly created park which had inspired its name – extended down the hill to the Wandle, bounded to the south-east by the high road to Rose Hill and Sutton, and on the west by a drive, now followed by a public road. Amongst the many trees and shrubs used to embellish and add interest to the gardens was a Dragon Tree, a botanical freak from the Island of Tenerife, brought back by friends from a cruise to the Canary Islands. Regrettably the three-storeyed house, large and decidedly ugly, failed to complement its setting and, with its red brick and tile, embellished with gothic detailing (the latter at Mrs Bidder's insistence), was reminiscent of a Victorian railway terminus.[40] It remained Bidder's property until 1877, when he transferred title to the whole of the Ravensbury estate to his eldest son, George Parker Bidder junior, for £40,000. Bidder senior and his wife moved permanently to another 'Ravensbury', on Paradise Point, Dartmouth, in his native county of Devon, where he died the following year at the age of 72.

George Parker Bidder 'the younger' (b. 1836) was admitted to the
tenancy of the manor of Ravensbury in 1859, when he was 21, but the
address of the property concerned has not been ascertained. He and
his wife Anna (née McClean), whom he married in 1860, were living at
Cedars Road, Clapham, when the decision was made to move to
Ravensbury. He was living there when he inherited the rest of the estate
following his father's death in 1878 and Ravensbury Park House was
to be his home for the rest of his life. George inherited much of his
father's brilliance. He obtained his master's degree at Trinity College,
Cambridge, graduating as 7th Wrangler. Electing to follow a career in
law, he was called to the bar at Lincoln's Inn in 1860. As Queen's
Counsel he acted for many railway companies and dock boards, and
practised at the Parliamentary Bar. Bidder, however, was a man of
many parts. He was involved in the founding of what became the Girls'
Public Day School Trust, was a justice of the peace and president of
the local Liberal party, the first councillor to be returned to represent
Mitcham on the newly created Surrey County Council at the election
held in 1889, and first chairman of Mitcham parish council in 1895. As
a churchwarden he was also a generous benefactor of the church, raising
with the help of friends the sum of £400 needed to reglaze the east
window in coloured glass of superior quality.

Bidder's Ravensbury Park House – postcard c.1910

Locally George Parker Bidder II is probably best remembered for his success in securing the preservation of Mitcham Common as a public open space, an interest he shared with his late father who, in the 1850s, had attempted in vain to secure the demolition of the disused parish workhouse on Commonside East and the return of its site to the Common. In the 1880s Bidder was in the forefront of the fight to save common land at Beddington Corner from enclosure for building. Success did not attend this particular effort, and after several hearings in the lower courts Bidder carried the case to the High Court but lost, and heavy costs were awarded to the defendants.

Eventually Bidder's dogged persistence carried the campaign to save Mitcham Common to a successful conclusion, securing the enactment of the Mitcham Common (Supplemental) Act of 1891 under which management passed to a Board of Conservators. Fittingly, George Parker Bidder became the newly-formed Board's first chairman. Tragically he died in February 1896 of injuries received in a street accident, and is commemorated by a granite monument erected on the centre of the Common, close to the Croydon Road. In Mitcham parish church his memory is kept alive by a tablet mounted to the right of the chancel arch, and by the brass lectern, presented by Anna Bidder.

Following Bidder's death discord surfaced in the family over the manner in which, in his capacity as executor and trustee of his late father's estate, he had handled affairs since 1878. There was no question of his having acted dishonestly, and at the heart of the dispute lay resentment that he had acted first without consulting his brothers and sisters. As a consequence, a law suit was brought against the executors of George Parker Bidder II's estate by certain of the beneficiaries, but the matter was settled out of court, and without lasting rancour. A result of the action, however, was that in what amounted to a forced sale the whole of the Ravensbury estate, comprising 167 acres of freehold land and nearly 67 acres of leasehold, was offered at auction. Particulars survive in the family's hands, but unfortunately the accompanying plan has been lost. A second sale by the developers occurred in 1901, of which particulars also survive together with plans, showing that the break-up of the park was proceeding, with the lay-out of the present residential roads to the south of the Wandle already established.

Ravensbury Park House and its immediate grounds remained intact, and eventually the house became the Catherine Gladstone Convalescent Home for women and children, the local directory for 1907 recording the proprietor as Mrs Gladstone and the matron as Miss Clara Bowles. In the 1930s the home had a complement of 46 beds, but it was badly damaged during the 'Blitz' and closed in 1940. Repaired, the house was re-opened by the Marie Celeste Samaritan Society as a home for the aged and infirm, but this, too, closed soon after the end of World War II and the building was demolished shortly afterwards. The site is now occupied by an estate of semi-detached prefabricated houses erected by the London County Council in the late 1940s and let to applicants on the housing waiting list.

Harold Francis Bidder, the second son of George Parker Bidder II, was born at Ravensbury Park on Christmas Day 1875. He obtained a degree at Trinity College, Cambridge, and then read for the Bar, being called at Lincoln's Inn. In 1899 he was commissioned in the Royal Sussex Regiment through the Inns of Court, and served in the Boer War with the third Battalion. His interests were wide, and included archaeology and music, as well as soldiering and law. In 1891 he commenced the

The Catherine Gladstone Home – The Garden – early 20th-century postcard

excavation of the Anglo-Saxon cemetery at Ravensbury, concluding his work in 1922 on his return from the 1914/18 War, in which he attained the rank of Lieutenant Colonel and was awarded the Distinguished Service Order. Harold Bidder continued his archaeological work in the district with the re-discovery of Merton Priory, and successfully campaigned for the site of the high altar of the priory church to be preserved and marked by a commemorative stone set in a small garden off Station Road, Merton Abbey. When the Merton and Morden Historical Society was formed in 1951 it was fitting that he should be invited to become its first president – a position which he had held for nearly 20 years when he died in Oxfordshire at the age of 92.

In about 1910 Harold Bidder commissioned the building of a new house, 'Ravensbury Manor', to the design of his brother-in-law Horace Porter and Percy Newton. The site chosen for the house, opposite what today is the junction of Morton Road and Wandle Road, together with part of the parkland on the north bank of the river, had been held back from the auction of his father's estate, and afforded a beautiful waterside setting. The house, which was finished in 1912, was conceived in the neo Queen Anne style popularised by Lutyens, with classical doorcases and a wealth of interior panelling, and stood on a stone balustraded terrace with steps descending to the water's edge. Here the Wandle, impounded by the mill downstream, formed a sheet of still water, mirroring the tall trees of the park beyond.[41] Regrettably Ravensbury Manor was to last barely 20 years, and in the drastically changed circumstances of the post-war years what remained of the family estate was soon covered with roads of suburban housing.

Two acres of land on the south bank of the Wandle downstream from Mitcham Bridge, known locally as 'Happy Valley' and originally part of the Hoare property, were donated to the National Trust in 1915 by Richardson Evans in memory of Octavia Hill. Two years before, 12 acres of watermeadow and osier beds on the opposite side of the bridge had been purchased by the River Wandle Open Spaces Committee and presented to the Trust. Together these two parcels of land now form the Trust's Watermeads property, and have the distinction of being amongst the earliest of the Trust's acquisitions.

Harold Bidder's 'Ravensbury Manor' c.1925 – reproduced by courtesy of Merton Library & Heritage Service

Some new housing, of a superior kind, had appeared in the vicinity of Wandle Road in the Edwardian period, but whilst the grounds of Hillfield House and the Gladstone Home remained intact, and open countryside extended to Rosehill and beyond, the setting of Ravensbury Manor must have seemed secure. A dramatic transformation was in the offing, however, and following the Armistice, building on this part of the Ravensbury estate began to gain momentum. The dwellings erected now were smaller, and many of them were individual self-build properties, constructed by their owners. The final blow was when, further to the south, a huge expanse of unspoilt farmland, some 825 acres in all and extending into Carshalton, was selected by the London County Council in 1926 for a vast new housing estate for inner London families.

Construction commenced in 1928, and was not completed until 1936. The architects of the new estate took full advantage of what was a classic 'green-field site', and planned the new cottage homes on the garden city principle. The name of the new suburb – St Helier – appropriately commemorated the efforts of Lady St Helier, a former alderman of the London County Council, who for years had campaigned for better housing for the poor of London.

Whilst there could be no denying the need for new housing, the rapidity with which former parkland and open countryside was now disappearing under the spread of suburbia engendered a reaction amongst those who remembered the district from their childhood, and wished to see the preservation of part of Ravensbury as open space and public recreational areas. In March 1929 the council of Merton and Morden Urban District was approached by the Urban District Council of Mitcham with the suggestion that the two authorities should join forces and purchase what remained of the grounds of Ravensbury Manor as a public park. Authority to borrow £5,500 had been obtained, and the London County Council had signified its willingness to contribute. A provisional joint committee was formed, and Merton and Morden Urban District Council was advised on 30 October 1929 that agreement had been reached with Mitcham, the purchase price being £5,310 and the expenses to be shared equally. Purchase was completed in November 1929, and formal opening of the new 16½ acre public park, 14 acres of which were in Mitcham, took place on the 10th May 1930, the ceremony being performed by George Lansbury MP, Commissioner of Works.[42] (Appendix 2: Plants in the park)

Shorn of its former grounds, and with its wider setting destroyed forever, 'Ravensbury Manor' was advertised in *The Times* in the early 1930s, but failed to attract a residential buyer. Demolition soon ensued, and the site was used for the building of maisonettes. The bellcote from the stable block was salvaged and installed atop the Cumberland Hospital, then being built behind Mitcham's Cricket Green, but this vanished in the redevelopment which took place in the 1990s. Only the former stable and garage block of Ravensbury Manor, converted into an attractive house at the corner of Morton Road and Wandle Road, survives to the present day.[43]

The 1930s saw the development of Ravensbury Park, the major part of which lay within the new Borough of Mitcham (the former Urban District had been granted municipal status in 1934). Formal flower beds became a much admired feature, a children's playground and paddling pool were laid out near the caretaker's house and adjacent café, and boating on

The Gardens, Ravensbury Park – postcard c.1960

the river became a popular summer facility. From Mitcham Bridge to Ravensbury Mill the more secluded sections of the Wandle banks became a haven for wild life, whilst in the vicinity of the rustic bridge giving access to the Morden side of the river ducks, swans, coots and moorhens gave pleasure to a generation of children taken with their parents to 'feed the ducks' with stale bread.

Sadly, during the 1939-1945 War and the years that followed priorities changed, and the park gradually declined. Ravensbury Park, along with many other parks in London and elsewhere, suffered from funding cuts during the closing years of the 20th century, resulting in loss of skilled workers. The proximity of the 1970s development of Octavia Close and Rawnsley Avenue had, and continues to have, an impact on the park, which the absence of full-time park keepers has exacerbated. Efforts are still being made, however, to improve access to the park and three new metal bridges within the park, of controversial design and practicality, were a recent project by Sustrans and Groundwork Trust. Sustrans with the GLA have designated the park as one section of a European cycle route, but the public conveniences have been closed due to vandalism.

One of the new metal bridges in Ravensbury Park – photograph D Roe 2005

Recently an area of the park near Morden Road, once occupied by the café and the children's playground, has been fenced off for the development of a medical centre, though construction has yet to start. A new play area is nearing completion in the 'bleaching fields', but without concern for its history. In 1996 and 1998 the council commissioned consultants to prepare reports on the park's character, conservation, history and restoration, but have failed to follow recommendations. The park's London Planes are huge, and it has the best Californian Laurel in London, the third best in England (confirmed by the Tree Register of the British Isles), but the latter is within the medical centre site, and efforts are being made to protect it. Recently many ornamental species, not suitable for the location or in line with restoration proposals, were planted as an arboretum.

Today a local amenity group, the Friends of Ravensbury Park, is active in the interests of the park and its users; the Tree Wardens regularly manage the woodland; and the Wandle Trust, who clear the river of rubbish, have helped the Friends remove invasive pennywort from the lake. Water quality is improving and angling is tolerated, as all sections of the community wish to see the park being used.

River Wandle, Ravensbury Park – postcard postmarked 1950

RAVENSBURY FARM

When the Ravensbury estate was offered for sale in 1855 it totalled 326½ acres, of which all but 99¼ acres were in Morden.[1] Although this is a Mitcham History, it would clearly be inappropriate to ignore 70% of the estate merely because it lies on the other side of the Wandle.

The Ravensbury lands in Morden were in three parts in 1855, the largest being 120½ acres of park and farm land included with the Manor House and its 12¾-acre grounds in Mitcham to form Lot One, purchased by George Parker Bidder I. Lot Two was the 93¾-acre Morden Farm, purchased by the sitting tenant, Henry J Hoare, who already owned and occupied the adjoining estate known as The Lodge, formerly Spital Farm. Lot Three was described as a "Villa Residence and Land", totalling 13 acres, purchased by the Revd Robert Tritton, rector of Morden from May 1835 until his death in November 1877, whose Rectory in Central Road was occupied by a curate.

Steel Hawes alias The Grange

The sales particulars describe the house that Tritton was to buy as follows:-

"THE HOUSE is Stuccoed and Slated, and contains an Entrance Porch and Hall; Dining Room, 22 ft. by 19 ft. 6 in. and 13 ft. 6 ceiling, with three Bow Windows, fitted, and walls papered; Breakfast Room, 19 ft. by 13 ft., 13 ft. 6 ceiling, three Bow Windows, walls papered; Vestibule; Library, 17 ft. by 18 ft. and 10 ft. ceiling, walls papered, with French Windows opening to a Verandah and Lawn; Drawing Room, 22 feet by 18 feet, and 10 ft. ceiling, walls papered, with same windows as last described and opening in like manner to the Lawn; Housekeeper's Room, Butler's Pantry with Sleepingroom adjoining, Footman's Pantry, Storeroom, Servants' Hall, Kitchen with water laid on, Dairy, Scullery, Wine and Beer Cellars, principal and back Staircase leading to nine Bedrooms, one Dressing Ditto, and two Servants' Rooms; two Water Closets, detached Coal House, walled in Yard, Coachhouse with two Bedrooms over, four-stall Stable with Loft over, Harness Room, Knife House, Wood Yard with Wood House, Brewhouse, Malthouse, and Toolhouse."

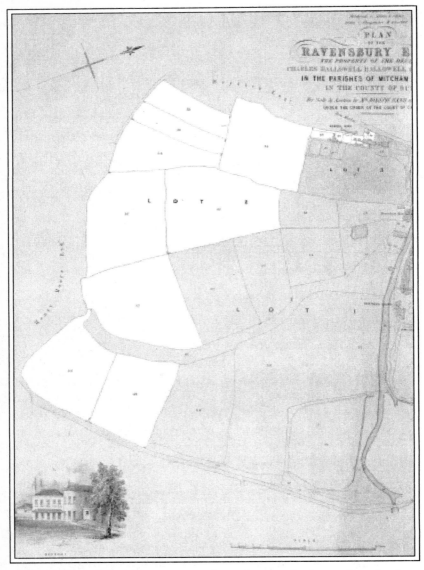

*Detail from the 1855 sales particulars, showing the Ravensbury lands
in Morden, reproduced by courtesy of Surrey History Service
Tritton's property is Lot 3 at the top right*

A drawing of the house is also included, with the caption "Rectory", as Tritton had been the tenant for the previous 23 years, paying the poor rate from July 1832, three years before becoming rector.[2] In the documents finalising the sale, the property was called Steel Hawes, from the name of the meadow in which it stood.[3] The fact that Tritton paid the poor rate is not proof that he was living at the property. In 1835 he appears for one year as lessee of another property in 'Morden Lane', that later known as Hazelwood.[4] As the poor rate for Steel Hawes increased by £10 in October 1835 it is possible that the family had found temporary accommodation while improvements were being made to the building.[5]

In 1878 Tritton's heirs sold it to Gilliat Hatfeild, lord of the manor of Morden since 1872,[6] and it was let to a succession of tenants. In 1915 Steel Hawes was opened as a convalescent home for soldiers, and from 1924 to 1964 it was occupied as The Grange Nursing Home, run by Edith Lewin until her death in 1941 and then by her daughter, Grace Minter.[7] Hatfeild's son, Gilliat Edward, sold the property to the London County Council in 1929 when the St Helier Estate was formed, and after 1964 it was used by the LCC and its successor, the Greater London Council, as a store for building materials required for the estate.[8] In 1971 Watney Mann Ltd considered turning the house into a two-bar pub and restaurant, but the costs of converting the building, listed as a building of special architectural or historic interest,[9] proved prohibitive.[10]

The Grange, Morden, before reconstruction, courtesy of W J Rudd
left: east elevation   *right: south extension courtyard*

In 1980 it was purchased by Courts the furnishing company for use as their company's headquarters building but, having suffered years of neglect and vandalism, the house could not be saved except for the shell of the north block. Surprisingly, Courts decided to rebuild it in replica, re-using suitable material from the old building wherever possible, and retaining the different floor levels of the original buildings. The replica building still stands on the corner of Central Road and St Helier Avenue, though at the time of writing it is vacant.

Fortunately an architectural survey of the original house was undertaken in 1965 by members of Merton Historical Society, who took detailed measurements of each room.[11] The GLC took photographs in 1966[12] and produced a report, which stated:-

> "... The Grange is considered as being of three attached blocks, one to the west facing onto Central Road, one to the east facing the garden, and one across the north ends of the first two. There are considerable out-houses to the south.

> "The earliest parts of the building are some of the timbers found in the west block. These timbers are re-used floor joists with chamfers and stops. Some are of large scantling, about fifteen inches, and are of medieval or sub-medieval origin. In one case at least the chamfering is on one of the upper edges, conclusively demonstrating that the beam has been re-used.[13] The west block was originally a timber-framed structure of three bays with brick-nogging. From the plan of the bays and the way in which the timbers were used it would be reasonable to suppose a date of erection in the late seventeenth century. It is impossible to say whether the earlier, re-used timbers came from the same site or not.

> "This west block was refaced along its west front at sometime in the eighteenth century with a two-storey brick wall faced in cement. This may have occurred at the same time as the second block, the east block, was built. This second block is of brick construction, not timber-framed.

"The north block built across the ends of the earlier blocks was probably constructed in the earlier part of the nineteenth century.
...

"... From the Tithe Map of the Parish of Morden it is clear that the Grange, including its out-houses to the south, was substantially the same in 1837 as it is today. From Rocque's map of c1768 it appears that only the west block had been built. It does not seem likely that the east block had been added, the map is not entirely specific on this point."[14]

Exploratory excavations carried out in the grounds by Merton Historical Society in 1972 recovered late-17th- and early-18th-century pottery, roughly contemporary with the first phase of building [see Appendix 4a].[15] No evidence of earlier occupation was found.

Morden Grange – WWI postcard

Ravensbury Farm

Until the 1820s this house had been the farmhouse of Ravensbury Farm. In 1823 C and J Greenwood mention "Ravensbury Farm in Morden, the residence of Thomas Merle, Esq.".[16] Merle had taken a sub-lease from Bernard Van Sandau in 1822, and four years later he took over the 42-year main lease.[17] Merle occupied the house and meadowland, while the farmland and farm buildings, together with a cottage "lately erected", were sub-let to George Glover.[18] In 1830 Mr Merle "became embarrassed in his circumstances" and went to live abroad. There being £470 due for rent and arrears, a distress was entered on behalf of Sir Benjamin Hallowell Carew, but there was not sufficient property on the premises to cover the rent. It was agreed that Merle (now residing in France) would give up the key to the mansion house and that Glover should pay direct to Sir Benjamin Hallowell Carew the rent due to Merle, and Glover should continue as tenant from year to year.[19]

Glover left in 1833, his departure giving rise to the following sale notice:

"Glovers Farm Morden

to be sold at auction by Messrs Fuller on the premises on Tuesday 13 August at 2 for 3 o'clock pm by order of the proprietor who had quitted the farm and left the county

The whole of the valuable crops of corn, grain and potatoes, comprising 25 acres of wheat with the straw, 18½ acres of oats with the straw, 24½ acres beans and the haum, about 1 acre of potatos [sic].

A very excellent timber-built and slated granary with 6 bins and standing on 9 stone caps; a few farming implements, and the fixtures in the house.

May be viewed the week preceding the sale, by application to Mr Thomas Billinger, the Bailiff, on the premises; and catalogues obtained at The George, Morden; King's Head, Mitcham; Nelson, Cheam; Bull's Head, Ewell; Bell, Merton; on the premises; and of Messrs Fuller, Auctioneers and Estate Agents, Croydon, Surrey.

Printed by J S Wright, High Street, Croydon."[20]

George Matthew Hoare replaces Glover in the Morden poor rate books from October 1833,[21] and it was his son, Henry James Hoare, who purchased the farm, then called Morden Farm, as Lot Two in 1855 for £4000.[22]

The land held by Glover and then by Hoare and the house held by Merle and then by Tritton had formed a single holding, Ravensbury Farm, until 1822. Described as a "mansion house and farm with appurtenances in Morden, part of Ravensbury manor" when the 42-year lease was granted to Bernard Van Sandau's predecessor, Edward White, in 1812,[23] its occupants can be traced back through Morden poor rate records to 1756.

Changes in the quarterly poor rate assessments may reflect structural changes. With each new tenant the assessment increased at first but, perhaps following an appeal, dropped a little next time. In 1813 Van Sandau was assessed at £300, a huge increase on the previous assessment of £167, though it dropped to £215 in 1814.[24] This could well have been due to structural enlargement, perhaps the northern extension. Similarly in 1802, White was assessed at £100, rising to £150 in 1804, before settling at £120 later that year, compared with the £75 assessment of his predecessor, Dantony Angell.[25] (White's 1812 lease was clearly not his first). Angel was assessed at £90 in 1787, though it fell to £60 before rising to £100 in 1788, dropping again to £80 in 1789, and settling at £75 in 1801, compared with the £53 of his predecessor, Christopher Chambers.[26] (Angell also held the tenancy of the adjoining Spital Farm from 1793 to 1803). Chambers, who also held the lease of the farm later known as Hill House, Morden, from 1778, had held the lease of Ravensbury Farm from 1768, in succession to Thomas Stacy, who was also tenant of the adjoining Duckett's Farm.[27] The assessment for Ravensbury Farm had fallen from £60 in 1768, following the transfer of some land from Ravensbury Farm to the adjoining Ravensbury Manor House estate.

John Arbuthnot's farm

This was the second transfer of land from Ravensbury Farm. The first had been negotiated in 1755 when, as we have seen in chapter 2, John Cecil, proprietor of a printworks at Merton Abbey, and his son-in-law John Arbuthnot, were granted a 99-year lease of Ravensbury Manor House and its grounds in Mitcham and Morden, including the Ravensbury printworks, then in the occupation of Thomas Whapham. At this time the boundary between the lands attached to Ravensbury Manor House and those of Ravensbury Farm seems to have been the curving tree-lined green lane known in 1838 as The Grove (Plot 41 on the 1855 sales particulars, plot 291 in the Morden Tithe Apportionment), which extended to the Wandle in the 1828 sales particulars map of Henry Hoare's estate,[28] and which still survives in part as Moreton Green. Arbuthnot's enthusiasm for agricultural reform has already been referred to in chapter 2, so it is not surprising that he wanted to extend his lands to take in some of the adjoining farmland in the occupation of Stacy, as well as some other Ravensbury land to the north-east of the estate, leased to

Farm buildings in Wandle Road, Morden, c.1952
reproduced by courtesy of Merton Library & Heritage Service

the neighbouring Mitcham Grove estate. In 1755 Cecil and Arbuthnot had agreed with Sir Nicholas Hackett Carew to lease up to 38 acres to be released by Thomas Stacy from the adjoining land he held of Ravensbury manor, and "the Ladyfield and Shaw" after the expiry of the current 39-year lease to William Myers of Mitcham Grove. However, Sir Nicholas died in 1762, before these arrangements had been legally implemented. Although Arbuthnot was paying poor rate "for Stacy land", valued at £15, from May 1760,[29] it was not until 1764 that the transfer of 37 acres from Stacy to Arbuthnot was agreed and confirmed by Carew's trustee.[30] No further mention was made of the land leased to Myers, but the Morden land tax records show that the owners of Mitcham Grove held some Carew lands until 1803.[31]

We have noted that the Ravensbury farm buildings were near Steel Hawes/The Grange in Central Road, so it is not surprising that there is no mention of any farm buildings standing on the land transferred from Ravensbury Farm to Arbuthnot. It is likely that the farm cottage and buildings included in Lot One of the 1855 sale particulars had been erected by Arbuthnot, or had replaced those erected by him. These included a fine timber-framed and weatherboarded barn that survived in Wandle Road until demolished in the early 1950s. Arbuthnot's farm remained part of the Ravensbury Manor House estate until 1827, when Henry Hoare of Mitcham Grove was granted a 21-year lease of these Ravensbury lands in Morden.[32] Sir John Lubbock bought the Mitcham Grove estate in 1828 from the heirs of Henry Hoare, together with Hoare's lease. Lubbock also leased Ravensbury Manor House. In 1855 Bidder bought all the Ravensbury land previously held by Lubbock, as part of his purchase of Ravensbury Manor House, and built his new home on part of it, as we have seen in chapter 2.

Little Steelhawes

The name Steelhaws was also given to a 3¼-acre meadow to the northeast of The Grange and separated from it by the road to Mitcham. The tithe map shows it surrounded by channels of the River Wandle, and containing a large rectangular pond, which survived until the 1960s, when it was deemed unsafe and filled in. The pond may have had ancient origins, as the name Steelhawes might refer to Old English *stiell*, a fishtrap or fishing-pool within a fenced or hedged enclosure.[33] In 1838 this meadow was owned by Richard Garth, lord of the manor of Morden,[34] but it had been part of Ravensbury manor until the 16th century. Following the Dissolution, the manor of Morden was sold in June 1553 to two merchants, Edward Whitchurch and Lionel Ducket.[35] Westminster Abbey, who had owned the manor of Morden from before the Conquest, had leased the manor to a 'farmer' for a term of 60 years from June 1511, and the Abbey's manorial centre, known as Munkton farm, was still occupied by the farmer.[36] Whitchurch moved into a "newly-builded mansion-house" on a copyhold property held from his manor of Morden, known as Growtes after an earlier tenant, in the grounds of the present Morden Lodge adjoining the Morden Hall Garden Centre. When he sold the manor to the first Richard Garth in March 1554, the estate also included a copyhold property in Morden "commonly called Stelehawes taken used or lettyn togither wᵗ the said house called Growtes".[37] This was presumably the "croft of land called Letle Steelehawes containing 3 acres of meadow in the parish of Morden in the manor of Ravensbury" formerly copyhold of the manor of Ravensbury, that Francis Carew, lord of the manor of Ravensbury, granted to Garth by indenture in February 1581 and confirmed by an "inrollment of feofment" at his manorial court in the following October.[38]

Duckets Farm

Lionel Ducket had also looked to the manor of Ravensbury for his home in Morden. In February 1585 Francis Carew sold to William Cowper 'a messuage or tenement with 12 acres in Morden, late in the occupation of Sir Lyonell Duckett, alderman of the city of London, sometime copyhold land of the manor of Ravensbury'.[39] In 1606 this property was sold to Lazarus Garth, one of the sons of Richard Garth, who in 1614 sold it to his brother, George, lord of the manor of Morden.[40] It was still being called 'Duckets Farm' in the 18th and early 19th centuries.[41] Thomas Stacy was the tenant in 1745,[42] and in 1770 Richard Garth leased it for 61 years to John Warrington, who held other leasehold lands in Morden.[43] In 1784 the lease was extended by 14 years and assigned to John Groves, owner of Growtes,[44] who in 1803 sold Growtes and the lease of Duckets Farm to Abraham Goldsmid the financier.[45] Goldsmid's executors assigned the lease to John Tyrrell in 1824, and he

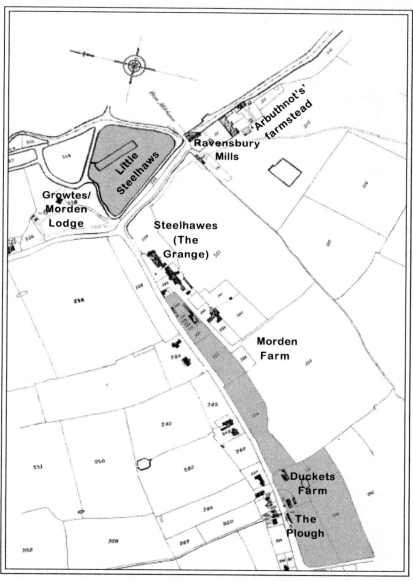

*Extract from an 1872 tracing of the 1838 Morden Tithe map, annotated
to show former Ravensbury property owned by Richard Garth
reproduced by courtesy of Merton Library & Heritage Service*

sublet it in three parts, the house in 6½ acres then being known as Poppendicks, after a former occupant.[46] Tyrrell assigned the main lease to William Henry Merle, son of William Merle late of Colliers Wood,[47] in November 1825,[48] and in 1831 Merle leased Poppendicks for 13¼ years to John Rutter, 'tobacconist', proprietor of Ravensbury mill.[49] In the Morden tithe apportionment schedule of 1838 a Captain Piper held the house, orchard and two paddocks totalling 6¾ acres,[50] the remaining land and cottages fronting Central Road being leased individually.[51] Three cottages had been built in the garden of Duckets Farm[52] and *The Plough* public house and an adjoining shop were built on a parcel of roadside waste nearby, enclosed in 1797.[53] These were all included in the sale when the house and orchard were purchased in 1866 by Joseph W Bazalgette, the engineer responsible for the London sewage system.[54] Five other cottages, part of Duckets Farm but adjoining Steel Hawes, were sold to Tritton at the same time.[55] Bazalgette was already resident in 1851, when the house was named in the Census return as Union Villa.[56] Later it was renamed The Willows, and Willows Avenue and the former Willows School site now occupy the site of Duckets Farm.

Origins

The origin of the Ravensbury estate in Morden is not known. The first clear indication that the forerunner of Ravensbury manor included lands in both Mitcham and Morden is found in 1321, when Florence and Philip de Orreby conveyed a substantial holding "in Mitcham and Morden" to William de Herle for life.[57] The two parishes are mentioned regularly thereafter in relation to the estate.

One intriguing feature of the estate that appears on the various 19th-century maps is a large oval enclosure of around 80 acres, bounded on its eastern edge by The Grove. The internal field boundaries are on a completely different orientation to those surrounding it, suggesting that it is a very early landscape feature, long pre-dating the surrounding field systems.

This chapter is based on a paper given by Peter Hopkins to a Merton Historical Society workshop in November 2007, with additional material supplied by W J Rudd.

THE RAVENSBURY PRINT WORKS

For possibly 300 years Ravensbury was one of three centres of the textile bleaching and printing industry which flourished on the banks of the river Wandle at Mitcham. The establishment of the bleaching industry in the London region is usually attributed to refugees from religious persecution in the Low Countries during the 16th and 17th centuries. An early Flemish presence in Mitcham is suggested by field names like 'Fleming Gate' and 'Fleming Mead' in use in the 16th century – the latter a water meadow on the banks of the river Graveney in the north of the parish.[1] Six 'strangers', whose names suggest Dutch or Flemish origins, were resident in Mitcham in 1592[2], and Adrian Collant, a 'whitster' or bleacher of cloth, who was buried at Mitcham in 1620, was described as "a Dutchman dwelling a long time in the parish".[3] There is also the enigmatic fragment of what was believed to have been a Flemish gravestone, discovered in a field near Ravensbury Park, some time before the 1914/18 War.[4]

Confirmation that bleaching was being carried on in the vicinity of Ravensbury in the late 17th century comes from the Quarter Sessions records, which show that William Wood, a whitster, was 'presented', i.e. summonsed, in 1690 for damaging the ancient common highway from Morden to Mitcham by making a watercourse.[5] Part of this 'highway' still exists as Ravensbury Lane, the cul-de-sac leading south from Morden Road between the park and the adjoining factories. Wood's watercourse was probably the forerunner of one of the streams which in the 18th century took water from the Wandle below Mitcham Grove and, after making a circuit of the lawns and shrubberies of Ravensbury House, served the bleaching grounds at the rear of what became the Ravensbury print works. It can still be seen today, as a stream running through Ravensbury Park near the Morden Road entrance.[6] As we have already observed, until the last century the remains of the parallel ditches of a long disused crofting, or bleaching, ground also survived as sufficiently conspicuous features in Ravensbury Park to attract the attention of surveyors working for the Ordnance Survey, and are marked on some of the larger scale editions of the maps until the 1930s.

The earliest records of fast dye cotton printing in England, to produce prints comparable with those imported from India, date from the late 17th century, a William Sherwin of West Ham, who seems to have pioneered the technique of madder printing in this country, being granted a 14-year patent in 1676. By the early 18th century prints in brown, black, purple and red were extremely popular both in England and abroad, and a thriving export trade with the North American colonies had developed. Difficulties experienced with mordants were overcome with the use of thickeners by the 1740s, and English printers by this time were able to produce multicolour patterns of great complexity and brilliance.[7]

The process of block-printing, and the equipment used, was described by Godfrey Smith in *The Laboratory; or, School of Arts* published in London in 1756:

> "Here the journeyman printer receives the prepared and calendered pieces ... He spreads it (the cloth) upon an oblong square table, of a considerable thickness, covered on the surface with a swan-skin blanket. Then taking the print in his right hand, and an oval mallet in his left, he dips the print on the colour, that

Engraving of a mid-18th-century calico printing workshop, from John Barrow, A New Universal Dictionary of Arts and Sciences *(London 1754)*

is spread by the tearing-boy, or girl, with a brush, upon a fine
worsted cloth, which is strained with a leather under it to a round
hoop-frame, and swims on dissolved gum that is in a shallow tub;
and then having thus furnished his print with the colour, he lays it
on the linen or cotton, and with the mallet gives it two, three, or
more knocks, according to the size of the print; then taking it off,
he repeats it, by observing the joining both at the ends and sides;
one table being done, he removes the printed work from off the
table, and thus proceeds with another, till the whole piece is done
... The pieces thus printed ... are from the printing shop conveyed
to the copper or boiling-house, where the copper-man, who has
the boiling of them under his care and management, puts them in
a large copper, and boils them with madder, a reddish drug."[8]

Peter Mauvillain, pre-eminent amongst the 12 calico printers known to
have been active in the Greater London area during the first half of the
18th century, claimed to have 205 workpeople employed at his works in
Mitcham and Wandsworth in 1719.[9] He had obviously achieved a
position of prominence in the industry some 20 or so years earlier, for
he was a signatory of the "humble petition" submitted to the House of
Lords in 1696, when a bill "for restraining" the wearing of "Callicoes
dyed, printed or stained" was under discussion, and was important enough
to be called to give evidence before the House of Commons in 1697.
The precise location of Mauvillain's Wandsworth factory has not been
established, but there can be little doubt that his Mitcham works were
at Ravensbury where, in his map of 1741-5, Rocque indicated a complex
of buildings. Moreover, Mauvillain was living nearby early in the 18th
century, having purchased the "mansion house" of Growtes in Morden,
in what is now part of the National Trust's Morden Hall estate.[10] This
was described as 'newly-builded' when sold by Edward Whitchurch
1554.[11] In October 1726 Peter Mauvillain purchased the Tudor house
from Thomas and Elizabeth Keene, the property being described as 1
messuage, 1 barn, 2 stables, 2 gardens, 2 orchards, 3 acres land, 3 acres
meadow, 3 acres pasture with appurtenances. The house, on the south
bank of the Wandle within Morden parish, is shown as "Mr. Movillians"
on a plan 'part of the River Wandel in the Parish of Morden' prepared
after a survey in 1750.[12] Ten years prior to the purchase, in October

1716, Peter and his brother Stephen had leased from Richard Garth's representatives part of the adjoining estate, later to be the site of the present Morden Hall. As well as the mansion house and outbuildings, and responsibility for maintaining "the Great Garden", the lease included 34 acres of land "and use, liberty, priviledge and benefitt of cutting and digging trenches, ditches and drains as they can and lawfully may grant in any part of these above mentioned premises (except the yard, etc.) in order to bring such part of the River Wandle as they the said Peter and Stephen Mauvillain shall think necessary or convenient, in, by or through the said premises for the carrying on of the trade, profession, occupation or business of staining, dyeing, washing and printing of calicoes or such other stuffes, goods, wares, commodities, matters and things as now are or hereafter may or shall be used".[13] Peter Mauvillain II still held this Garth leasehold property in 1745.[14] It is thus in St Lawrence's churchyard at Morden that we find the tombs of Peter Mauvillain, Stephen Mauvillain and his son, another Peter, dated 1739, 1740 and 1755 respectively.[15] Peter junior was described as a plate printer in an indenture of 1738,[10] and in 1753, his father and uncle having died, he sold Growtes to Philip Selby of Carshalton, a whitster, in January 1753.[16] All of these gentlemen, we may assume, had close connections with the family business founded by Peter senior.

The size of Mauvillain's workforce, and its concentration in factories, is an interesting feature of the enterprise, for Mauvillain was pioneering aspects of the industrial revolution normally associated with the latter part of the 18th century. Unlike the production of woollens, which was still organised on a domestic basis, the successful importation, processing and marketing of the finished calicoes called not only for the investment of considerable capital, but also for organisational skills of high order. In their evidence before the commissioners of trade and plantations in 1720 the printers emphasised the heavy outlay in buildings, the diversion of water and laying out of grounds, plus investment in expensive machinery to which they were committed before production could start. Again, unlike the traditional cottage-based woollen industry, the printing of linens and cottons called for a co-ordination of many skills, and Mauvillain is said to have had 152 hands working in one factory alone, bringing together the crafts of fieldmen, 'tierers', grounders and printers, drawers and cutters.[9]

As we have seen, there are various references from the mid-18th century to John Arbuthnot, the first calico printer known for certain to have been connected with the Ravensbury factory, and it would seem that he took over the Mauvillains' business, possibly shortly before the death of Peter Mauvillain junior. The land leased by Arbuthnot from Carew in 1755[17] lay in both parishes, on either side of the Wandle, and it seems highly likely that it had been held previously by Mauvillain, although this cannot be confirmed. Arbuthnot's first marriage was to Sally Margaret Cecil, daughter of John Cecil of Abbey House, Merton, proprietor of the calico printing works founded in the former priory grounds in 1724.[18] The grave of Mrs Hannah Cecil, his mother-in-law, who died at Merton Abbey in January 1756 aged 58, is marked on a low table tomb in Morden churchyard, and John, 'of Ravensbury', who died in April 1760, was also buried at Morden. Bequests in various wills show that the Cecils and Mauvillains were related by marriage, and a more detailed examination of the partnership of the two families can be found in Peter McGow's paper 'The Ravensbury Printing Works, Mitcham' deposited with the Wandle Industrial Museum, and available on their website.

Whereas initially Arbuthnot was involved personally in the production at the Ravensbury works, after the death of his wife Sally in 1759 and his father-in-law the following year, his interests had clearly extended to high farming. By 1761 the works are shown in the Mitcham poor rate books to have been in the occupation of Thomas Whapham,[19] who undertook various improvements to the Ravensbury factory, and in 1763 created a tumbling bay and dam on the river for which he became responsible by indenture.[20] From this we may deduce that he was acting in his own right under a sub-lease. It is, of course, possible that Arbuthnot, as head lessee, retained some interest in the enterprise, but this is conjectural, and research by McGow shows that by the late 1770s Arbuthnot was in financial difficulties, probably an outcome of the American War of Independence and disruption of trade with Britain.

The embellishment of textiles with colours capable of withstanding washing was achieved by the use of mordants, metallic compounds which react chemically with dye. The dye most commonly used was obtained from the root of the madder plant which, although naturally of a reddish hue,

when used with different mordants (from the French *mordre*, to bite),
would produce a range of colours. The method followed in mordant-
madder printing, which ensured that only the patterned part of the calico
retained the colour, was to print the fabric with the mordant, and then to
uniformly dye the whole of the piece being processed. Subsequent exposure
of the cloth to sun and air bleached out the dye from the untreated portion,
leaving the desired pattern on a white ground. Experienced dyers could
produce a great variety of colours and shades by their choice of mordant
and by manipulating the strengths of the solution applied.[21]Arbuthnot
experimented with the cultivation of madder at Ravensbury, and there
is a suggestion that a mill on the Morden, or southern, bank of the Wandle,
was being used in the 1760s for the grinding of dyewoods, another source
of colour, but the building had been converted to snuff milling by 1790,
when it was in the hands of William Fenning.[22]

In 1780 the Mitcham land tax records list a new occupier of the
Ravensbury calico print works – Thomas Hatcher, who held a house
and lands valued at £100 p.a. for tax purposes. The 'proprietor' of the
land was Richard Gee Carew, Sir Nicholas's heir. By 1779 John
Arbuthnot's relative, Admiral Marriott Arbuthnot, was in residence at
Ravenbury House, and from this point on the histories of the house and
the print works diverge.[23] Hatcher's "neat white house" lay on the same
bank of the Wandle as the old manor house, but about a furlong (200 m)
to the north-west, and downstream. The prints produced by Hatcher
were evidently highly regarded – a contemporary refers to him as "a
gentleman much noted for his manufactory in the callico line"[24] – and
he would appear to have taken over at Ravensbury in immediate
succession to Thomas Wapham. Unfortunately Hatcher's tenure was
to be of short duration, for he died in 1787; his standing was such that
his passing merited a note in the *Gentleman's Magazine*.[25] The house
overlooking the river remained in the occupation of his widow for a
year or so, but by 1791 it had become the residence of William Fenning.

Thus we find the Ravensbury works in the hands of William Fenning
"of Merton Abbey" who had, in fact, paid poor rates for premises
elsewhere in the parish of Mitcham as early as 1769, and whose firm,
Fenning and Company, had been renting land near the Ravensbury
factory in the early '80s. Like Hatcher, Fenning had previously been

manufacturing at Merton, the first indication of his involvement in the calico printing industry being in the will of Jonathan Meadows of Merton Abbey, thread whitster, dated December 1778, in which Fenning is styled "Mr. William Fenning of Merton in Surrey calico printer".[25] Very wisely, it transpired, he took out a fire insurance policy with the Royal Exchange in March 1791 to cover the "utensils and stock" and the timber-built, tiled-roofed water-mill at Ravensbury for the sum of £100.[26] Two years later the author of *Ambulator* observed, after noting that Fenning had grounds for bleaching and printing on the banks of the Wandle at Ravensbury, "Mr. Fenning has an engine in case of fire, the pumps of which are worked by the same wheel that is used in the business. He experienced the benefit of this machine a few months ago, when his premises took fire, and would have been totally consumed but for this admirable invention."[27]

William Fenning ran the Ravensbury works for over 20 years before his death in August 1812, at the age of 74. He was buried in Mitcham churchyard, where the inscription on his tombstone affords him the style of 'Esq'.[28] His son, also named William, inherited the business but, either lacking his father's enterprise, or perhaps finding the returns from block-printing insufficiently rewarding in the face of competition from the new roller-printing methods being employed at the Merton Abbey works and elsewhere, he relinquished his interest shortly after the end of the Napoleonic War. The flurry of arming and drilling which followed the renewal of hostilities with France in 1803 had seen the formation of 'The Loyal Mitcham Volunteer Infantry' in which William Fenning junior served as captain of the first company.[29] His lieutenant was Robert Wasley, whose son John was to become manager of the Ravensbury factory some 40 years later. (Robert Wasley, described as "Drilling Master 50 years", died 1 June 1842 aged 82 and lies buried with his wife Mary and daughter Sarah in Mitcham churchyard.) Fenning resided at Baron House, a substantial property in Lower Mitcham, until 1807 and then moved to Christ Church (Southwark) where he died in February 1837. He was buried in the family vault at Mitcham.[25]

Bailey Austin, who followed the Fennings as the proprietor of the business at Ravensbury, was granted a 21-year lease in 1817. The premises were described as "that Messuage or tenement with Mill Houses, Buildings, Stable and Appurtenances at or near Ravensbury" and land called the "Whitstring alias the Whitening Ground, 10a 1r 10p and 2a 27p abutting".[30] The ivy-covered tomb of Bailey Austin, described in his will as "calico printer of Ravensbury, Mitcham," can be seen in the parish churchyard. He died in 1823, leaving bequests to his parents, John and Sarah Austin of Oundle. Another new name, that of Frederick Benjamin King, 'calico printer', Austin's brother-in-law, now appears as the occupier of the Ravensbury works over the next five years, following Bailey Austin's death.[31] Bailey Austin had been associated with the Ravensbury factory for some time, possibly as a partner of William Fenning the elder, with whom he was of an age. As we shall see later, the development of partnerships in the calico printing industry, in contrast to ownership by one person, does seem increasingly to have been a feature of the structure of those businesses surviving into the middle of the 19th century. King carried on after Austin's death, but by 1828 had been succeeded by Edward Walmesley. Further research by McGow has clarified the situation, which is complex, for these men were operating in a period of acute post-war depression, and in the face of growing competition from the steam-powered mills of the industrial north.

With the appearance of Edward Walmesley on the scene at Ravensbury around 1827[32] we enter a new and what seems to have been the last successful period in the factory's history, extending over 14 years.[33] Walmesley had come to live at Morden in a house in Central Road, later known as Hazelwood, and was still assessed on it in the land tax records when they ceased in 1831.[34] Perhaps significantly, he seems to have been the last of the proprietors to have lived close to the works, and was thus in a position to exercise personal supervision. In August 1831 he was granted a seven-year under-lease of "All those mill houses, drying houses, sheds and buildings now and for several years past used by the said Edward Walmesley as a factory for carrying on the business of a calico printer" by John Jonas Child of Hadley.[35] Child was probably acting on behalf of Hugh Arbuthnot, the head-leaseholder, who was by now a major-general and member of Parliament for Kincardineshire.[36] On the other hand, Child could have represented either Austin's

Undated watercolour by William Wood Fenning (1799-1872), son of William Fenning junior, showing the Ravensbury Printworks, possibly painted during a visit in 1850, reproduced by courtesy of Sue Wilmott

beneficiaries or King's creditors. Actual ownership of the land was still in the hands of the Carew family of Beddington, and a review of mills on the Wandle in 1834 shows the print works, leased and occupied by Edward Walmesley, as being in the hands of the late Sir Benjamin Hallowell Carew's executors.[37] The lease included not merely buildings, but also fixtures, machinery and utensils, leaving Walmesley to provide mainly labour and materials.

In August 1836 Edward Walmesley surrendered the uncompleted term of his under-lease to Arbuthnot and negotiated a fresh lease of the messuage with mill house and land (the description confirms that this included the "Whitstring or Whitening Ground" mentioned in previous deeds).[38] On the strength of his extended tenure he obtained fresh working capital secured by a mortgage for £4,750.[39] For four years all seems to have gone reasonably well, and as 'Walmesley and Co. – Ravensbury Factory' the firm is listed under 'Calico, Silk etc. Printers' in a local directory of 1839.[40] For a brief period Walmesley enjoyed a reputation for the manufacture of Paisley-patterned shawls, then an essential element of fashionable attire for ladies, but fashion is fickle, and the good times did not last.[41]

It makes little demand on the imagination to visualise the widespread social effects of the steady decline in the local textile industry which had been a feature of the local economy, albeit with brief intermissions, since the 1820s, leading to closures and often bankruptcies. A notebook kept in 1837/8 by one of the curates at Mitcham parish church, the Revd Herbert Randolph, contains several references to Edward Walmesley and also to Samuel Makepeace (another calico printer who had a factory in Willow Lane). An elderly block printer, William Hersey, is said to have been "badly off from the state of trade", and of Henry and Charlotte Thompson, Randolph recorded "26 weeks out of work. Son nearly 21 no work for the last 8 months. Badly off." The monetary wages of those parishioners fortunate to remain in work are given in several instances, and of course appear extremely low in comparison with modern expectations: "William Upham, widower ... son is married and ... works at Walmesleys, receives 10/- or 12/- per week ..." and "Foster Edwards ..., works at Mr. Walmesley's at from 15/- to £1. 5. 0 per week" (presumably a skilled man).[42]

Edward Walmesley died in about 1840, but the firm continued for a while. The census of 1841 found Mary Walmesley, then in her mid-fifties, living at the house adjoining the works, with John Wasley, the manager of the calico factory and his wife nearby, and in another house connected with the works, John Berryman the manager of the copper house and calico ground, also with his wife and family.[43]

The mortgage raised by her late husband was surrendered and extinguished by Mary Walmesley in 1842 with, one suspects, money raised by the sale of her interest in the business.[44] From now on the financial difficulties being encountered by the new lessees of the works become woefully evident. The precise reasons for their recurring failures have yet to be ascertained, but changes in fashion, a contraction of demand for the more expensive English hand-printed fabrics, competition from the increasingly industrialised manufacturies of the Midlands and north of England as well as imports from the Far East – all probably contributed to the hard times experienced by the manufacturers in the Wandle valley.

In 1845 the *London Gazette*[45] gave notice of a fiat in bankruptcy dated February of that year against Lawrence Daniel Dolbell, a dyer at Ravensbury Mills, and five years later, in March 1850, came the formal announcement of the dissolution of the partnership between Edward Carter and John Downing, "Silk, Woollen, Challi [Challis] and Fancy Printers at the Willow Mills and Ravensbury Mills".[46] All debts due and owing were to be addressed to Carter. On 6 December 1850, the *Gazette* published notice of the dissolution of the firm of Carter, Bowen and Co, silk, calico and shawl printers, and the following August the hearing of the adjudication of bankruptcy filed against Owen Bowen and Alexander Gibson of the Ravensbury Print Works, both of whom were described as calico printers, was set for the Court of Bankruptcy on 13 September 1851.

The records of the tithe survey of 1846/7 give only the name of John Geary, a dyer, as occupier of the printing factory and its associated buildings,[47] and the census of 1851 lists him as works manager, living on the premises. As the resident manager, he was presumably endeavouring to maintain some form of production whilst his employers struggled to weather the financial storms that beset them.

John Arbuthnot's original lease expired in 1854, and in July the following year, when the Carews' Ravensbury Estate was in the process of being broken up, the Ravensbury factory came up for sale.

 The buyer was Peter Dempsey who, with his partner George Heard, had actually been in occupation of the works for several years. The conveyance of the Ravensbury Print Works, described as a "house and certain premises now used as a shawl and linen printing manufactory with certain grounds attached thereto and which was formerly used as a Calico manufactory ..." with 14 acres 10 poles of land, is dated December 1856, and names Charles Hallowell Hallowell Carew of Beddington and others as the vendors, and Peter Dempsey and his trustee as purchasers.[48] The plan accompanying the conveyance shows the premises to have comprised all the land lying between the river, Morden Road and the western boundary of the grounds of Ravensbury House.

Under the proprietorship of Dempsey and Heard, shawl printers, the Ravensbury Print Works were now to enjoy a final, albeit brief, period of activity, if not actual prosperity. Ben Slater, in his memoirs of Mitcham in the middle of the century, said of "The Ravensbury Factory":

> "... this was noted for calico printing, also silk printing, and the noted Paisley shawls were made and printed here to a large extent. There were a great number of hands employed here, both men and women, French, Scotch and English."[49]

Braithwaite, visiting the area in the spring of 1853, had observed that

> "Below Mr. Gifford's grounds [i.e. the grounds of Ravensbury House, now Ravensbury Park] are the print works of Messrs. Dempsey and Hind [sic], which employ one wheel of 8 H.P.; the mill head is 46 feet 7 inches above T.H.W.M.. This firm used half a carboy of sulphuric acid weekly; [only one sixth the consumption of the Phipps Bridge Works downstream] a carboy or about 8 gallons of muriate of tin per month [1/12th the consumption of the Phipps Bridge Works] 5 cwt. of prussiate of potash, and 5 cwt. of oxalic acid per annum; also a certain quantity of sulphate of copper, nitrate of iron, chloride of lime etc, all of

which materials are discharged into the river. Moreover, the works require, for the washing of goods, all the water that can be obtained, and four men are constantly employed in rinsing them in the stream. The deep, colouring matter may be observed for more than 200 yards."[50]

The basic process employed at the Ravensbury works by Dempsey and Heard probably differed little from that described in 1814 by Edward Bancroft as being used by the printers in New England. Two or three pounds of madder for each piece of calico were crumbled in water, which was then brought to blood heat. The pieces of calico, previously printed with various mordants and then joined together, were thoroughly immersed in the dyeing liquor about an hour, care being taken to ensure the cloth was continuously agitated and completely impregnated with the dye. The length of material was then quickly removed and thoroughly washed in a stream of running water to avoid spotting. Next it was boiled with bran to remove any remaining madder residue, and spread on the grass of the crofting grounds to bleach in the sun. If necessary the boiling with bran and exposure to sunlight were repeated until all trace of the madder dye had disappeared from the parts untreated with mordant. The metallic mordants used were in themselves colourless, but were capable of producing fast colours in various shades of rose, brown, purple and so on in the finished article.[8] There can be little wonder that at Ravensbury, where the washing process was virtually continuous when the works were in production, the Wandle was highly coloured below the point at which the effluent was discharged.

As we have seen, below Mitcham Bridge water from the Wandle had, for perhaps two centuries or more, been diverted into an artifical watercourse which meandered through the grounds of Mitcham Grove and Ravenbury House, before ultimately reaching the Ravensbury works. Within two years of the sale, a dispute had arisen between Dempsey and a Mr Hitchcock, the new lessee of the house, over the pollution of the river caused by the works effluent.[51] Its effects on the fine trout still to be caught in the Wandle at this time was certainly a matter of concern to those with interests in angling, and 'The rise and fall of the River Wandle' was the subject of a paper presented to the Institution of Civil Engineers by Braithwaite in 1861.[50]

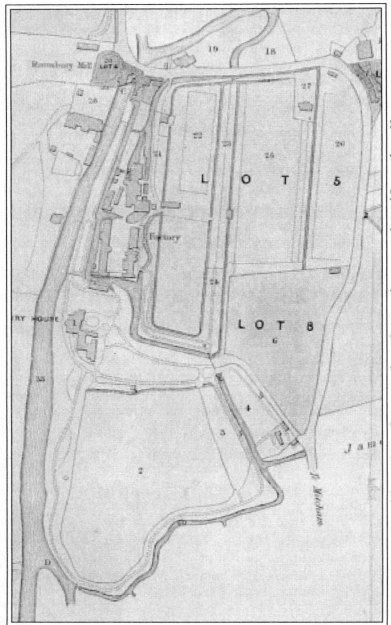

Detail from 1855 sales particulars, showing the printworks and Ravensbury House reproduced by courtesy of Surrey History Service

By now, however, the works were again in trouble. The partnership between Peter Dempsey and George Heard "as shawl printers or otherwise" at Ravensbury Print Works, had been dissolved in April 1856,[52] and whereas the reasons for the split are unknown, it is clear that in the years that followed Dempsey was continually pressed for money. It seems likely that it was to finance the business and meet his debts that £2,500 was raised by mortgage in February 1857, and a further £500 in December 1858.[53]

Further loans were arranged with William Simpson of 'The Manor House', Mitcham, between January and May 1861, and a second mortgage was raised with Simpson in July to enable Dempsey to meet interest payable,[54] but this relief failed to save the business, then obviously in terminal decline. The end came in August 1862 with the sale to William Simpson by Sumner and Holt, Dempsey's mortgagees, of a cottage and a little over six acres of ground lately occupied with the print works.[55] Once again, one glimpses the social stress which was the inevitable consequence of this collapse of an industry on which many families had relied for a century or more. The Revd Daniel Wilson, newly instituted to the vicarage of Mitcham in 1859, was deeply concerned at the distress and poverty he found in his new parish. He was particularly saddened by the hardship experienced during the severe winter of 1860/61, writing in his pastoral letter "... much distress is caused among the poor by the demand for labour being so small. Before the introduction of steam, the various factories were in full work, now short time is too often the case. The printers are, by reason of their employment, unfitted for hard work, and they live on, buoyed up with hope, too often a delusive one, of getting work in the factories."[56]

The Ravensbury Print Works, the cottage and ground were mortgaged for £3,400 by Simpson immediately on purchase, and then let to James Wilkinson of Sydenham for one year at £300.[57] Wilkinson, unfortunately, died within a few months, and the agreement was annulled in February 1863.[58] Simpson and his mortgagees next conveyed the old print works and associated lands to James Terry and James Whitehead of London, who mortgaged the property for £6,600 for a year.[59] By 1874, after further mortgages had been raised, Henry Hoare of Hoare's Bank had become the landlord, and the factory and premises had been let for one year to

Lamprell, Andrews and Emerson, lace merchants.[60] A year later, in February 1875, Hoare granted them a lease for 9 years.[61] The following April, he sold the whole of the property to Gilliat Hatfeild of Morden Hall. The property by this time comprised a water-mill and manager's house, the factory (with the manager's residence), the *Ravensbury Arms*, 1-4 Morden Place, some cottages in Ravensbury Grove and Ravensbury Road, further building land, and Ravensbury Cottage.[62]

During the inter-war years the present *Surrey Arms* in Morden Road replaced an old inn and row of early 19th-century weatherboarded cottages, part of the former Carew estate, and a small block of shops was built in the Morden Road adjoining a new *Ravensbury Arms* (now replaced by a block of flats) at the corner of Ravensbury Grove, but the general atmosphere was still essentially rural. The lace manufacturer's lease of the Ravensbury works terminated in 1884, and the factory had almost certainly closed down before the turn of the century. The old buildings remained, however, gradually becoming more and more derelict but still sufficiently intact in the 1940s to be used for storage. The millpond and numerous watercourses also survived, although much overgrown by rushes and willows and, by operating the valves controlling the flow of water, the wheel could still be made to turn. (See Appendix 3)

Postcard of The Surrey Arms, Morden Road, c.1910

Under the Hatfeilds' ownership little material change was to occur in this part of Mitcham until after the 1939-45 war. Giving a talk on 'Old Mitcham' in 1933, the 83 year-old Walter Hunt, dubbed "One of Mitcham's grand old men" by the local press, recalled "Ravensbury, the most charming part of the whole district" around the time of Hatfeild's purchase as:

> "... not yet disfigured by the factories now standing in Morden Lane. Harvey and Knight's floor cloth factory, which had been but recently built, was scarcely in sight from the river, upon whose banks the kingfisher and moorhen used to foregather with a certain amount of security, and beautiful trout grew to full size in the water.

> "For a time we lived in a house beside Rutters' snuff and tobacco mills, which were driven by two large waterwheels on the Wandle. Our fairly large garden at the back extended along the river bank, and in a punt built by my father my brother and I used to row upstream under picturesque overhanging trees into what seemed to us fairyland. The thrills experienced on these occasions were sometimes called to mind many years later when cruising amongst even more beautiful surroundings on other parts of the World."

In the 1980s deeds of the Mitcham Rubber Co's former factory premises in Morden Road, covering the period 1856-1916, were deposited at the then Surrey Record Office by British Telecommunications plc, following their acquisition of the premises.[63] These show that the site, a piece of freehold land called Finning Field amounting to 3 acres and situated near Ravensbury House, was once part of the Carew estates. The land was purchased in 1876 from the auctioneer V J Blake of Croydon by Daniel Hayward and Sons Ltd, another firm of linoleum and floor cloth manufacturers. Despite being built of brick, Hayward's linoleum factory met with disaster several times through fires. The aftermath of what was probably the last fire, whilst the premises were still in Hayward's ownership, was photographed by Tom Francis, and is reproduced as plate 156 of *Old Mitcham* (1993).

Following Hayward's declaration of bankruptcy in 1887 the site was bought by the Mitcham Linoleum and Floorcloth Co. Two years later ownership passed to the British and Foreign Oxolin Co, who in turn sold the factory and land to Messrs Bigby, paint and varnish manufacturers, in 1901. The subsequent conveyance of the site to the British Rubber Co in 1916 includes a plan showing details of the layout of Bigby's varnish works at that time. The 1932/35 OS map shows the eastern corner of the site, abutting Ravensbury Lane, as the 'Imperial Works' of Hancock and Corfield, manufacturers of enamelled signs, etc. The rubber works continued to occupy the adjoining site until the 1940s, when they were destroyed during an air raid. In 1965 the corner site was still occupied by Hancock's, then known as Hancock, Corfield and Waller, whilst the former rubber works was used as a pipe store by the GPO telephone department.

The Hatfeild estate in Mitcham and Morden was offered for sale by auction in May 1946. Damage caused by flying bombs towards the end of World War II had left the buildings of the Ravensbury print works in a ruinous condition, and the site was purchased for housing purposes by Mitcham Borough Council. The first dwellings erected were a row of prefabricated concrete houses in Morden Road, facing the park entrance. Site preparation necessitated backfilling the ditches once running across the bleaching grounds, and the work was carried out by Italian and Austrian prisoners of war. A later phase in the development of the new estate in the early 1950s involved the demolition of the cottages in Ravensbury Grove and The Laurels, a late Victorian red brick house at the corner of Morden Road which had been leased by Hatfeild in 1904 to Thomas Harvey, a varnish maker, and let to William Marshall, whose family occupied it for many years.

Inevitably the clearance work also included the ruins of the old print works, and very little now remains to guide the interested visitor to the site of the factory. There is a short length of 13½-inch red brick boundary wall facing the river, and a backwater winding its way round the edge of Ravensbury Park to join the Wandle below the mill pond of Ravensbury Mills, but both are meaningless without a plan of the works in their heyday. Today, lock-up garages at the side of No. 11 Ravensbury Grove occupy the site of the manager's house, whilst the roads and gardens of the post WWII Council estate cover the bleaching grounds.

The Ravensbury Printworks in 1890
reproduced by courtesy of Mrs Madeline Healey

The cottage occupied by Hatfeild's bailiff, the last remaining building contemporary with the works on the northern, or Mitcham, bank of the river, stood beside a roadway giving access to the factory from Morden Road. Its low-pitched slate roof and walls of yellow stock bricks indicated erection in the earlier part of the 19th century, and the building is shown on the 1846 tithe map, but nothing much is known of its origins. It was included in the Carew estate sale of 1855, and it was one of the cottages acquired by Gilliat Hatfeild in 1876. Abram Clark, the bailiff for the Morden Hall estate, lived there for many years, followed by his stepson, William Williams. Williams also worked on the estate, having been employed by Gilliat Edward Hatfeild since his boyhood, and became bailiff himself after serving in the 1914/18 war.

When the Hatfeild estate was auctioned in 1946, William Williams as a sitting tenant successfully bid for his cottage, encouraged by the assurances received that Mitcham Corporation did not require the property. Within a year or so, however, the Council placed a compulsory purchase order on it, buying at the favourable auction price and not the current market value.

The Bailiff's Cottage with Mr & Mrs Williams in 1959
reproduced by courtesy of Mrs Madeline Healey

Mitcham's redevelopment plans did not necessitate demolition of the
cottage, and after his retirement William Williams was allowed to retain
the tenancy, and lived to reach the age of eighty. The long narrow garden,
bordered by a leat from the mill pond, was beautifully kept by the old man,
and created a brilliant splash of colour in the early summer with peonies
and irises in profusion. By 1959 Surrey County Council had finalised their
plans for diverting the river above Ravensbury mills as part of a
comprehensive scheme of flood control, and it was obvious considerable
changes were in the offing. Work commenced towards the end of 1962,
and the still picturesque setting of Ravensbury cottage was destroyed,
breaking old Mr Williams's heart. He died of pneumonia early in 1963,
and three years later the cottage, empty and becoming increasingly
dilapidated and a prey to vandals, was demolished. It could have been
sold and renovated, but the Council decided that the land on which the
building stood was needed for access to the newly installed flood control
gates. The site of the cottage and its garden have now been incorporated
in the riverside walk forming an entrance to Ravensbury Park.[64]

Two of the names for the roads on the new municipal housing estate
were chosen for their local associations – Hatfeild Close, and Rutter

Gardens, the former recalling the last lord of the manor of Morden and the latter commemorating the Rutter family, manufacturers of snuff and tobacco at the Ravensbury Mills for over a century, whose 'Mitcham Shag' acquired a nationwide reputation. Regrettably the opportunity to acknowledge the even longer history of calico bleaching and printing at Ravensbury was missed, probably because it was all but forgotten by the time the land was redeveloped in the immediate post-war period.

Quite by accident, however, the estate revived a connection with the Low Countries dating back 400 years, for one of the roads was named after the Dutch township of Hengelo, twinned with the Borough of Mitcham at the end of the 1939-45 War. The link is commemorated by a metal plaque set in a concrete slab at the roadside, inscribed

"Hengelo Gardens,
30th August 1952
This plaque was unveiled by
the Burgomaster of Hengelo
as a token of the friendship
between the people of Mitcham
and Hengelo in the Netherlands".

The plaque in Hengelo Gardens in 1980

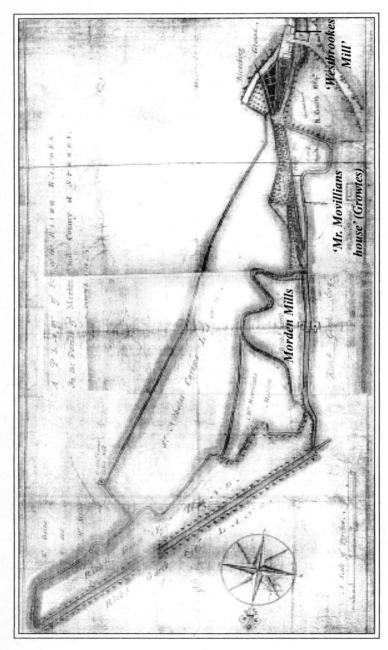

'A Plan of Parts of the River Wandel In the Parish of Morden and County of Surrey. survey'd 1750'
reproduced by courtesy of Merton Library & Heritage Service

THE RAVENSBURY SNUFF MILLS

The Domesday Survey of 1086 recorded two mills within the future civil parish of Mitcham, and on the basis of what is known (or can be deduced) of their subsequent history neither seems to have been located at Ravensbury. Another mill was also recorded at Morden, but its site has not been identified.[1] The de Mara or de la Mare family, who held the manor of Ravensbury through much of the Middle Ages, certainly owned a watermill, but there is good evidence to show that it was not situated at Ravensbury, but a little over a mile downstream, beyond Merton Bridge.[2]

What seems to be the first mention of a mill on the Wandle at Ravensbury occurs in the manorial rent roll recording that a rent of £5 was paid to Sir Nicholas Carew by a Mr Westbrooke for a "newly erected mill below Ravensbury house". The roll is undated, but the handwriting, and what is known of the history of the Carew estate, has led the County Archivist to ascribe it to the 1680s.[3] It is conceivable that the document may actually date to either 1688, when Francis Carew inherited the family estates on the death of Sir Nicholas, his father, or perhaps the following year, when Francis himself died, heavily in debt. The subsequent family dispute over guardianship and management of the Carew properties culminated in litigation, as a consequence of which matters were placed in the hands of the 'punctilious' Charles Bynes of Carshalton, acting as official receiver.[4] It was noted in the rent roll that the amount payable by Westbrooke had been increased to £6 10s, which conveys a hint that at around the time the roll was compiled the financial administration of the Carew estate was being placed on a more realistic footing – probably by Bynes.

Nothing in the rent roll indicates that the new mill replaced an earlier structure, and the Ravensbury Mills were paying tithes in the 19th century,[5] which implies that the site was not that of a mill 'of ancient demesne', with origins in the Middle Ages, and therefore free of tithe. We are thus left to conclude tentatively that construction of the mill should be dated to within a decade or so of the Restoration. Nothing seems to have been recorded to suggest the identity of the entrepreneur responsible being other than Westbrooke himself, and the purpose for which the mill was first used is not known.[6]

A 'Plan of Part of the River Wandel In the Parish of Morden and County of Surrey Survey'd in 1750' for Richard Garth, owner of the Morden Hall estate, indicates, probably in stylised form, a large rectangular building or group of buildings astride the river in the position now occupied by the Ravensbury Mills, plus a smaller building adjoining, on the north or Mitcham bank of the mill-head.[7] Against the latter structure, but probably relating to the whole complex, is written "Westbrooks Mill". The earliest surviving Mitcham poor rate book, for September 1755, lists a Mr Busick as the rate payer in respect of a mill and land, assessed by the parish overseers at £15 per annum, which he rented from Sir Nicholas Carew.[8] There is no indication of what Busick was using the mill for, but the following February, when the rate book no longer mentions Busick, there is a new entry for "Mr. Arnold's snuff mills", valued at £32.[9] This doubling of the rating assessment almost certainly reflects enlargement of the premises by Arnold on taking over from Busick.

In October 1758 Latham Arnold, described as "of Newgate Street, Tobacconist", insured his mill on the Mitcham bank of the river with the Hand in Hand insurance company. The policy was renewed in 1765, 1772 and 1779.[10] In March 1765, when the valuation for rating purposes was increased, this time to £63, the entry "Mr. Arnold for Mill and land late Busick" makes it clear the same premises are involved. By 1769 the assessment had risen to £82 [11] – a change which, once again, must reflect the continued expansion of the premises stimulated by the profits to be made from snuff manufacture. From the insurance records it is evident that Latham had an interest in another mill at Ravensbury, situated on the Morden bank of the river. In 1761 and 1768 this was described as milling logwood (from which dye was extracted), but by the time Arnold renewed cover in 1775 both mills had been converted to the grinding of tobacco for snuff.

It is apparent from the map produced for Richard Garth in 1750 that mill buildings were already straddling the river, which here formed the parish boundary. Whilst the rates demanded by Mitcham steadily increased over a period of a decade and a half, the Morden overseers appear not to have shown the same level of interest, and their records seem somewhat inconsistent.[12] From 1780 onwards, however, the premises were assessed for Land Tax in both Mitcham and Morden concurrently. The implication is that the mill at Ravensbury was established initially on the north bank of the river, and that expansion on to the Morden bank took place gradually during the third quarter of the 18th century. Prentis[13] noted on a visit to the mills in the 1960s that the floors of what he believed to be original buildings on the north bank were below the level of the water in the mill pond outside. The slate-roofed and weatherboarded buildings he saw may not, in fact, have been as old as the 17th century, but the floor levels certainly indicated that they pre-dated the creation of the large mill head we can see today.

It is from the last decade or so of the 18th century that we begin to have other evidence which confirms that the snuff mills buildings were becoming concentrated on the Morden side of the river. Edwards's map of c.1789[14] for instance, marks a "Snuff mill" on the south bank, although not at the roadside as today. An ink and blue wash sketch of the rear of the mill made by James Bourne in about 1810, makes it quite clear that the premises then comprised a group of buildings disposed across the end of the mill-head, with a subsidiary grouping of smaller

*Ink and blue wash sketch of the rear of the mill by James Bourne c.1810
reproduced by courtesy of John Turner*

buildings on the Mitcham bank.[15] There were also two wheels in parallel, very much as at the Morden Hall snuff mills today, and a tumbling bay discharging on the northern side of the mill pond as it did until modified in the early 1960s. Wilfred Prentis[16] was evidently pursuaded by Rocque's map of 1762, which marks a snuff mill at Ravensbury, to conclude that the mill building fronting the road today was "probably" already standing in the 1760s. Bourne's drawing, which depicts the buildings as gabled and with an irregular roof-line, quite unlike the large yellow stock-brick structure surviving to the present day, shows that Prentis was misled.

Peter McGow's work on the insurance registers has enabled the history of Latham Arnold's snuff mills to be followed in some detail until his death in 1781.[17] His daughter Mary married the Revd John Pearkes, whose brother Martin entered into partnership with Latham in about 1777, and it was from Martin Pearkes that the snuff and tobacco business was acquired by John Rutter of Love Lane, Aldermanbury in 1805. During Pearkes's time the premises were extended, an indication that the business was prospering, and in 1789 there is mention of insurance cover being granted for a newly erected warehouse opposite the snuff mills, and a barn situated some 20 yards to the east. In September 1790 Pearkes (still trading from the premises in Newgate Street) took out a fire insurance policy with the Sun Insurance on the utensils and stock in "A House, Water Snuff Mill" and adjacent shed at his factory at Mitcham. At the same time he insured "an adjoining House and Tobacco Mill House", together with a warehouse, in Morden.[18] These were the buildings depicted by Bourne, and are shown by the policies to have been of timber construction, with tiled roofs. They were insured for £500 and £1000 respectively, and the two water-wheels and machinery were valued separately at £500. Pearkes and Company did not actually own the premises, but held them by lease from Richard Gee Carew of Beddington, who had come into the family estate in 1780 on the death of an aunt.[19]

An archaeological evaluation conducted by the Museum of London Archaeology Service in October 1992, when an application for planning consent to redevelop land at the rear of the Ravensbury Mills was under consideration by the London Borough of Merton, exposed several features to support the belief that the earliest buildings had been on the north bank of the river.[20] Here, in one trench, the remains of a large wall of red unfrogged bricks was uncovered. This had been built in a timber-revetted foundation trench, and was dated to "perhaps" the 17th or 18th centuries, and could well have been part of Westbrooke's mill of the 1680s. In a second trench, also on the Mitcham side of the river, several arched brick channels were found, believed to have been constructed to control the flow of water beneath a building. Again, construction materials suggested a date contemporary with the late 17th-century mill. On the southern, or Morden bank, a distinctive feature in the one trench opened by the archaeologists was a buried river channel which, until it was levelled with dumped material, seems likely to have formed a major depression on this side of the river. The clay and sand filling of the depression contained fragments of the same early red bricks found on the north bank, and could well have been deposited here when the level of the mill-head was raised in the latter part of the 18th century. This may have taken place in the 1780s when, as we shall see below, there seem to have been new buildings erected on the Morden side of the river or, alternatively, shortly before the erection of the present mill building early in the 19th century.

Although the use of tobacco, taken in the form of snuff, had been widespread on the Continent in the 17th century, it did not become fashionable in England until the reign of Queen Anne, and it was another 50 years before snuffing ousted the smoking of tobacco in popularity. The elegant use of snuff gradually evolved into a social accomplishment and extravagant claims were made for its alleged therapeutic properties. To meet the demand, production in this country greatly expanded in the 18th century, though the best quality snuff, and hence the most expensive, continued to be imported from France and Portugal. Prices varied enormously, and the varieties were legion. The process of manufacture took up to 20 months to complete, and involved the grinding of the tobacco, for which water power was used, and repeated fermentation. Snuffs were perfumed with jasmine, cloves, lavender and attar of roses, the two latter being produced in increasing quantities by the Mitcham physic gardeners towards the close of the 18th century. By this time snuff milling had become an important local industry, there being three mills operating on the Wandle above Mitcham Bridge, plus the Ravensbury Mills, and two more in the grounds of Morden Hall. There were also others upstream, in Beddington and Carshalton.[21]

Edwards, collecting information for his *Companion from London to Brighthelmston* in about 1788, describes "a snuff mill belonging to Mr. Spencer", as being about a furlong downstream from Ravensbury,[22] but Spencer's name does not appear in either the poor rate books or the land tax records, and it is thus a little difficult to relate him to the premises held by Pearkes. One can only assume that he occupied the premises on a sub-lease or some form of tenure under which he was not responsible for rates and taxes.

A plan of the Wandle through Richard Carew's estate, drawn in 1804 following a survey conducted by the Croydon surveyor William Lazonby, survives in the London Borough of Lambeth's archives at the Minet Library.[23] Lazonby shows "The Manufactory of Martin Pirks Esq." occupying buildings astride the river, with a frontage on the Morden Road. The ground plan of the principal building corresponds so closely with that of the main component of the Ravensbury Mills today, and the materials used and the style of construction are so evidently of the early 19th century,

Ravensbury Mill from Morden Hall Road (ENM 1968)

that one can be reasonably confident in asserting that Pearkes and Company had demolished the old timber and tiled buildings a short while before the survey. In their place had been erected the large building which, apart possibly from a new roof, the steel trusses of which seem more likely to date from the late 19th century, survives virtually intact on the Morden side of the river today. The fact that the assessment of £72 for land tax in Morden remained unaltered from 1800 to 1832 gives support to the conclusion that the building dates from the very end of the 18th century.

As we have seen, in 1805 the Ravensbury snuff mills were taken over by John Rutter, who had founded a tobacco and snuff manufacturing business in the City of London 15 years previously. In December 1805 he was joined in partnership by his two nephews, Thomas and John.[24] The family had roots both in Mitcham and Morden, the marriages of two Rutters being recorded as early as 1738 and 1746 in the two villages respectively. In the late 1780s a Robert Rutter (d.1815) occupied part of a house in the nearby lane (now Central Road) leading to Morden as a boarding school "for young gentlemen",[25] and for the next 150 years the parish registers record the baptisms, marriages and deaths of numerous members of the family, several of whom, as might be expected, took an active part in local affairs. In about 1816 Thomas Rutter built Morden Lodge (now owned by the National Trust) and lived there until his death in 1821.[26] His brother also dying in 1821, their business interest was devolved to their cousin, John Rutter III, who was in partnership with his uncle Isaac. The name of the firm was changed from J Rutter and Company to Isaac Rutter and Company after Rutter senior's death.[27]

The actual ownership of the land was soon to pass into the hands of Sir Benjamin Hallowell Carew, but the Rutters continued to hold their premises, which included gardens, a meadow and a barn in what is now part of Morden Hall Park between the river and the *Surrey Arms*, on a lease.[28] Isaac Rutter died, aged 59, in 1837 and was buried at Morden. The firm continued for another quarter of a century in the control of the third generation partnership of John Rutter III and Isaac Campbell Rutter [29] and, later and briefly, James Rutter. The sale of the Carews' Ravensbury estate in 1855 brought the mills on to the market, and the Bidder family papers have a record of George Parker Bidder acquiring the lease of the snuff mills in 1856.[30] By the 1880s the great grand-nephews of the firm's founder had come into the business, Hugh Campbell Rutter and Henry Crofts Rutter being the principals, and so the story continues, until Rutter and Company left Mitcham in about 1925.

The mid-19th century probably witnessed the climax of snuff milling at Ravensbury. In 1853 the combined output of the two wheels equalled 21 horse power,[31] and since at this point the full potential of the Wandle could be impounded in the Ravensbury mill-head, a constant source of water was assured. The tail-race flowed under the road outside the mill, and was joined in Morden Hall Park by the overflow from the tumbling bay on the mill pond and two small backwaters from the Ravensbury print works. In addition to the snuff mills, the Rutters rented on the Mitcham side of the river some 33 acres of meadow and gardens, plus various buildings and yards, from Captain Charles Hallowell Carew.[32] By this time the family had several branches, some living in Morden (the mill house demolished in 1994 was one of their homes) and others in Mitcham at Raydon, in London Road, one of the Baron Grove houses and Glebelands, off Love Lane, and, from the 1890s, in Mostyn Road, Merton Park.

In response to changes in fashion and demand towards the end of the Victorian era Rutters turned increasingly to the manufacture of tobacco for the cigarette and pipe smoker, their 'Mitcham Shag' being a particularly well-known line. Snuff milling, however, continued to be an important activity at the Ravensbury Mills until they were finally closed down. Some contraction seems to have taken place in the second half of the 19th century, for when Gilliat Hatfeild, the new squire of Morden, acquired a leasehold interest in part of the Ravensbury mills in 1884, it was said that they had been used between 1868 and 1884 as a flock mill by James Thomas Roe, a shoddy (shredded re-used cloth) and flock manufacturer and broker, and later by William E H Hooper who, with his wife, lived at Morden Lodge for a short time in the mid 1870s.[33]

The final commercial occupiers of the Ravensbury mills, Whitely Products Ltd, were first included in the local directories in 1925.[34] The firm had been founded by an American in 1894, and manufactured a great variety of sports goods and athletic equipment, rubber cords, and such diverse items as starting gates for horse races, luggage straps, chest expanders and exercise equipment, bungee cords for stunt men, and arrestor gear for aircraft carriers etc.[35]

In the autumn of 1959 plans were produced by Surrey County Council for modifications to the various backwaters of the Wandle above Ravensbury Mills as part of the authority's Wandle Improvement Scheme. Flooding at vulnerable points throughout the valley had been causing serious problems for some years, and at Ravensbury the proposals were for the abolition of the old tumbling bay and overflow channel, and the construction of a new automatic tilting gate discharging into a 22-feet-wide spillway through what hitherto had been the garden and orchard of the cottage on the north bank of the river. At the same time the sides of the mill-head were to be strengthened with new retaining walls of sheet steel piling, but the mill-tail beneath the road was to be left intact. The works were completed in the early 1960s, and, as far as can be seen, were carried through in their entirety.

Today the two cast iron breastshot wheels, mounted in parallel, are still to be viewed, housed behind doors within the main mill building. Their metal L-section blades are practically intact, and the wheels were last

The rear of Ravensbury Mills (ENM 1994)

used to drive wood-turning machinery, but by the 1960s they ceased to be utilised as a source of power. Inside an adjacent workroom there was a large wooden drive wheel mounted on the axle of one of the water-wheels, together with parts of other machinery, formerly connected with belting.[36] Although the bearings were badly worn, the wheels were still capable of being turned, and periodically the sluice gate controlling the flow of water to the central channel of the mill-race was operated to allow wood and accumulations of other rubbish to be washed into the mill-tail and pass away downstream.

In January 1970 the local press caused some alarm by reporting that, although it was no longer used as such, the future of the mill had been placed in jeopardy by road widening proposals, which would do away with the tail-race. These came to nothing, and the Morden Road at this point remains constricted to two lanes, and, although a pelican crossing has been installed, it is still dangerous to pedestrians attempting to cross from one side to the other.

Around 1980 the Ravensbury Mills were vacated by Whitely Products Ltd, and the buildings remained empty for some 14 years. During this time they were broken into repeatedly, and at least one fire severely

The overflow from the mill pond (ENM 1992)

Ravensbury Mills. Water-wheel assembly 1970

damaged the older buildings on the Mitcham side of the river. With the future of the site uncertain, these were not repaired, and the mills and the detached mill house remained vacant, a prey to vandals, and increasingly derelict as a consequence.

The wheels at the Ravensbury mills were included in the 1965 edition of the Surrey County Council's *Antiquities of Surrey*, and their historic interest has quite recently led to their being afforded the protection of a Grade II statutory listing.[37] In 1992 the Council of the London Borough of Merton granted planning permission for the redevelopment of the site, including partial demolition of, and alterations to, the mill buildings and their use after restoration by the Wandle Industrial Museum. The remainder of the site, on both banks of the river, was to be used for the erection of residential accommodation. Modified proposals were submitted by the architect late in 1993 and approved, and works were commenced in September by Fairclough Homes Ltd. Within five months the first of the new flats was occupied, and repairs to the wheels were being undertaken by the Wandle Industrial Museum, to whom part of the mill buildings had been offered for display purposes. Details of tenure have yet to be resolved.

The water-wheels at Ravensbury Mills
Merton Borough News photograph January 1970

WHITE COTTAGE, MORDEN ROAD, MITCHAM

Arguably one of the most visually attractive of the National Trust's domestic properties in the London Borough of Merton, White Cottage, or Casabianca,[1] in Morden Road is also a rare example of a three-storeyed tiled and weatherboarded house. This form of construction was once common throughout north-east Surrey and Kent, and of course still dominates the vernacular architecture of New England, but the ravages of rot and woodworm, exacerbated by neglect, have combined with a mania for development to reduce those left in the Greater London area to a mere handful.

Stylistically, White Cottage must date from the latter half of the 18th century, and a building is indicated on the present site in Edwards's map of *c.* 1789.[2] Its precise date of erection has not been ascertained, but some time between perhaps 1760 and 1780 is feasible, and of the three local builders active in Mitcham at this time Samuel Oxtoby seems most likely to have been responsible for its construction.

Early in the 19th century White Cottage became the residence of William Ness, a gentleman of independent means.[3] Tenure of the property was by lease, with ownership being in the hands of the Carews of Beddington. Ness died in 1844 at the age of 84, and a white marble tablet to his memory can be seen on the wall of the south aisle of Mitcham parish church. He was survived by his wife Eliza, who was some 30 years his junior, and she stayed on at White Cottage for another ten years or so.

With the break-up of the Carew estate White Cottage (described as a "freehold cottage residence" and still occupied by Mrs Ness) was bought in 1856 by Samuel Haines.[4] The following year he sold it to Henry Haines, an auctioneer and surveyor,[5] who at that time was living with his family at The Rectory, a substantial house standing in extensive grounds overlooking Cranmer Green, Mitcham. Henry Haines relinquished tenure of The Rectory in the mid-1860s, apparently moving away from the village, but White Cottage, leased to tenants, remained his property until his death in around 1873.

In 1875 Haines's widow leased White Cottage to Robert Ellis of Elm Lodge, which overlooks the Cricket Green at Mitcham, and he purchased the property four years later.[6] Ellis, who was a mineral water manufacturer, sank an artesian well at the rear of White Cottage, where he built a small factory and offices. His 'Raven's Spring' (the name was obviously inspired by the manor of Ravensbury or the nearby Ravensbury Park) is marked on a map of 1883[7] and in another, dated five years later, the factory is shown, measuring 54 feet by 25 feet, together with the well and a 'well room'.[8] The seemingly unlimited supply of wholesome, albeit hard, water was a valuable asset, but the premises were small and by 1882 the business must have been transferred to the Ellis family's larger Ravenspring Works in Western Road, Mitcham, for in this year White Cottage and the buildings at the rear were purchased by Gilliat Hatfeild of Morden Hall.[9] A cast-iron drinking fountain fitted with a chained metal cup, which presumably had been installed by Robert Ellis for the benefit of passers-by, remained in the front garden for a number of years but, like the inscription it once bore, has long passed beyond living memory.[10]

From the time of its purchase by Gilliat Hatfeild, White Cottage has been a private residence and part of the Morden Hall estate, passing into the ownership of the National Trust in 1942 following the death of Hatfeild's son, Gilliat Edward, in 1941. During the 1939/45 War, when an ammunition dump was located to the rear of the premises, the old factory building was used as a Home Guard post. Nothing of this remains, but the house fortunately survived the war, shaken during the air raids but relatively unscathed, and was categorised by Mitcham Borough Council as Grade III in the supplementary list of buildings of architectural and historic merit prepared under the provisions of the Town and Country Planning Act of 1947. It was subsequently upgraded, and is now Grade II in the statutory list compiled by the Secretary of State.[11]

Repainting was carried out by the National Trust in the autumn of 1980 after overhaul of the structure, but White Cottage stood empty and boarded for several years more before a new leaseholder was found, prepared to undertake further refurbishment and maintenance necessary to ensure the continued survival of the property.

White Cottage, Morden Road (ENM 1995)

above: 'South West View of Mitcham Grove'
below: 'South East View of Mitcham Grove'
Watercolour drawings by J Buckler dated 1818
reproduced by courtesy of Merton Library & Heritage Service

MITCHAM GROVE

An Introduction

According to contemporary topographical writers,[1] a remarkable feature of Mitcham in the late 18th and early 19th centuries was the number of gracious country houses and elegant villas to be seen within the boundaries of the parish. None, however, could compare with Mitcham Grove, for 42 years the home of Henry Hoare, a member of the celebrated family of Fleet Street bankers. This beautiful residence, probably one of the finest houses ever erected in Mitcham, and certainly the largest of which record survives, stood on slightly elevated ground on the north bank of the Wandle some 60 yards west of Mitcham bridge. Surrounding it were lawns, gravelled walks and over 20 acres of parkland planted with a great variety of shrubs and exotic trees. The setting alone would have ensured Mitcham Grove a place of distinction amongst the other property in the district, quite apart from its association with several prominent figures in the history of British politics, finance and social reform. The origin of the house itself is obscure, although documentary evidence lends support to the theory that it replaced or even incorporated within its structure elements of an earlier house which, in the reign of Elizabeth I and for a century and a half afterwards, was the home of one of the leading families in the village. Excavations conducted by Surrey Archaeological Society on the site in 1974/5 demonstrated that Mitcham Grove itself had been preceded by another substantial house, probably the centre of a complex of domestic buildings, which had been occupied in the 14th and 15th centuries.[2]

An important clue to the early history of Mitcham Grove, to which we have referred earlier, may be contained in the conveyance of 1362, by which William Mareys or de Mara of Mitcham leased his house and land in 'Wykeford', including two water-mills on the Wandle and marshland adjoining 'Beneytesfeld', to the Church.[3] Constituent elements of this extensive estate can be identified in later records. The mills were located just upstream from today's Mitcham bridge; Beneytesfeld can be shown to form part of Poulter Park on the south bank of the river; whilst Wykeford, or 'Whitford' as it is rendered in Domesday

Book, is synonymous with Lower Mitcham. Much of the property, known as 'Maresland' was held by Merton priory until the 16th century,[4] when it was granted by Henry VIII to Robert Wilford, a Merchant Taylor of London.[5] William Mareys remained an important personage in Mitcham for a decade or so after making the estate over the Church. No records relating specifically to the house have survived from the intervening two centuries, and the site of his 'capital messuage' has been lost. It is tempting, however, to conclude that the footings of a medieval building exposed beneath Mitcham Grove in 1974/5 were, in fact, the remains of Mareys's house. Circumstantial evidence points to much of his former estate, including what survived of the house, having passed into the possession of Thomas Smythe by the latter half of the 16th century.

The Smythe Dynasty (1564–1725)

The early years of Mitcham Grove may be obscure but, as we have seen, there are good grounds for believing that here, on a slightly elevated position on the banks of the Wandle, a substantial medieval building was replaced in the 16th century by a fine new house, erected for Thomas Smythe, an official in the court of Queen Elizabeth I. In the 1870s biographical research was undertaken by Robert Garraway Rice on people whose names appear in the earliest Mitcham parish registers, which date from the late Tudor period. Results of his work were published in *The Reliquary* in 1877, and include details of the Smithe or Smythe family, who first appeared in the registers during the mid-16th century. Rice noted a reference in the baptismal register of 1590 to "Mr. Smythe's howse by the Watersyd",[6] and was aware that when the family returned their pedigree in the armorial visitation of 1623 their crest was a buck's head.[7] He also recalled that when Mitcham Grove was demolished in the 1840s the same heraldic device had been discovered painted on ancient panelling until then hidden behind battening and canvas, and he concluded that the house, or parts of it, had once been in the possession of the Smythe family.[8]

One of the earliest entries in the registers records the baptism in August 1564 of Edward Smythe, "the natural sonne of Thomas Smythe esquire one of her majesties servantes". Smythe's first wife was Mary Cely (or Sely), about whom nothing else seems to have been recorded. Another son, George, who was to inherit the estate, was born around 1561 and had, presumably, been baptised elsewhere. The note of Edward's christening, the first of many entries chronicling the births, marriages and deaths in what became one of the leading families in the village during the next 260 years, is followed in quick succession by others recording the baptisms at yearly intervals of brothers and sisters born, one assumes, on the correct side of the counterpane.

Thomas Smythe's second wife, Elener, was of the family of Hazelrigge, or Hesilrige, but the date of their marriage is unknown. His fortunes were evidently already in the ascendant when, in 1569, he purchased from John Swyfte of London the lordship of the manor of "Downesforth alias Donnesforthe [i.e. Dunsford] and a messuage called the garrett within the parish of Wandsworth".[9] At this time Smythe was also busily assembling an estate in Mitcham, purchasing freehold property from William Stevens in 1567, Richard Stappe in 1571, and Christopher Stewarde and Thomas Wylforde in 1574.[10]

The precise service Smythe rendered his queen is not clear, but he is styled in one genealogy as "clarke of ye Greencloth".[11] The Board of the Greencloth was a department of the royal household which in Elizabeth's day had control of various matters of expenditure, besides legal and judicial authority within the sovereign's court-royal. Of Smythe's antecedents we have no information. When he died he held the lordship of a manor in Wiltshire, and it is tempting to believe he may have been related to the great Thomas Smythe, the yeoman's son from Corsham, Wiltshire, whose immense proficiency and financial acumen ensured the success of Burghley's experiment in the farming (or, as we would say, privatisation) of customs administration. Despite his contribution to Elizabeth's exchequer, 'Mr Customer Smythe' did not receive the honour of knighthood from the Queen. He succeeded, however, in amassing a fortune rivalling that of many members of the peerage, into which his grandson Viscount Stangford took the family.[12] Customer Smythe outlived his namesake in Mitcham, and at his death his eldest surviving son bore the name of John. There is a possibility that Thomas Smythe of Mitcham was a son or nephew, but this remains to be explored.

Thomas Smyth(e) of Mitcham was unquestionably a man of standing in the world of his day, possessing a considerable estate. In his will dated 1575 "in perfect mind but sick of body", he left to his wife Elener[13] for life two thirds of all his "lands in England", which included in Mitcham three messuages or houses, 20 acres of arable land, five acres of meadow, four acres of pasture, with their appurtenances, besides other property at Wandsworth and Streatham. Elener was also willed use of all goods, furniture, plate etc. in his house at Mitcham, with the proviso that should she remarry this was all to go to his son George. There was a specific exclusion of a silver and gilt "bason" and ewer, two silver spoons, the best silver salt, and a gilt silver tankard, which seem to have been left to George personally. George was also bequeathed "a gold chain, a gold ring with arms thereon, bedstead and household stuff in a chamber in Black Fryers, London, a chamber at Court, "game of swans" (i.e. the right to take swans for his table) "on the River of Ware and game of swans on Mytcham River". Smythe's will also names his other children, Edmund (to whom was left the manor of "Mounton-farlyt" in Wiltshire), Mary (who was married to Edward Brabazon), Edward of Wandsworth, Eleanor and "Mary Smythe the younger". Servants were left sums of money, and there were the customary bequests to the church and poor of Mitcham.[14] No maps of this part of Mitcham survive from the 16th century to indicate the position of Smythe's house, but notices served on riparian owners by the drainage authority in 1572[15] make it obvious that his estate bordered the Wandle between the Watermeads and what is now Ravensbury Park. To the east of the house his property included a field immediately to the south-west of Mitcham mill, tenanted by a John Woimanne. To the west, the estate seems to have been bounded by "longe poole lane", as yet not identified with certainty, but most likely the ancient highway leading to Morden from the vicinity of Mitcham church, adjacent to and also passing through today's Ravensbury Park.

At the time of his death in 1575 Thomas Smythe was in "debte, daunger and bonde of twoe thousand poundes", and the prospects for George, his eldest son and heir, then a boy of 14, seemed bleak. The following year Elener Smythe remarried, taking as her second husband Bartholomew Clerk. The choice proved a fortunate one, for Clerk redeemed much of Smythe's property, including the latter's "choice house and Landes", to which he had no title in law, and eventually made them over to his stepson George. Clerk, a fellow of Kings College, Cambridge, doctor of civil law and dean of the arches, held the lordship of the manor of Clapham, and it was to Clapham that he took his wife. In 1584, at the time of a dispute between Sir Francis Carew and Lord Howard of Effingham over the extent of the manor of Ravensbury, Clerk's estate, held in right of his wife, included some 30 acres of 'Marrish' land, two water mills, and a house in Lower Mitcham.[16] The building of the manor house at Clapham, at which Queen Elizabeth was entertained in 1583, is attributed to Clerk,[17] and at his death in March 1590 he directed that he be buried in the north chancel of Clapham parish church. Elener died four years later and was buried near him.[18] "George Smythe gentleman" receives regular mention in contemporary records. He married Rosa Worsop of Clapham and, if we are to be guided by his will, his career seems to have been attended by even greater financial success than that of his father. He resumed residence at the family house in Mitcham well before the end of the century, and "Mr. Smythes howse by the Watersyd" is mentioned in the Mitcham parish register for 1590 as the birthplace of a child fathered by William Daunce, but whether the mother was there as a resident or visitor is not stated.[6] Smythe is known to have also kept a house in Mugswell Street, London, but the nature of his business interests is unknown. It is to be hoped that affairs in London did not prevent him enjoying the pleasures of his country estate, enhanced in 1595 by a grant of free fishery in the Wandle downstream from Phipps Bridge by the lord of the manor of Biggin and Tamworth.[19]An indication of George Smythe's standing in the County is afforded by his appointment by the Queen's Commissioners in 1593 as High Collector of the Lay Subsidies in the Hundred of Wallington, although comparison of the assessments given in the subsidy rolls would imply that he was not yet one of the major landowners in Mitcham. At 20% the tax he paid on this occasion – 20 shillings on lands valued at five pounds – was heavy enough, but it was probably levied on the net value only. The valuations were, of course, to a large extent arbitrary, and their main use to the local historian is as a means of assessing relative wealth.[20] In 1625, when loans were extracted from the more substantial gentry in Surrey for the benefit of Charles I, George

Smythe contributed £20. Towards the close of Elizabeth's reign Smythe (like his father before him) was active in enlarging the family's estate, and in February 1594/5 purchased from "Henry Whitney of Micham esq. and Anne his wife" four acres in Carshalton parish adjoining a mill house. This land was described as "part of Mareslande or Maresfee, the estate of the dissolved 'monastery' of Merton", and was obviously near the river, but its precise location is uncertain.[21] At about the same time Smythe also purchased from Whitney another parcel of freehold land in Mitcham, together with other freehold land from Alice Tyler and William Travys.[10] In addition to the mills he inherited with his late father's estate, George had evidently acquired a third by 1610, for in a list of flour mills on the Wandle compiled in that year three are shown to have been in his possession.[23] The third mill was probably that noted in a survey of the manor of Reigate dated 1623, which found that as a freeholder

> "George Smyth, gent., holdeth also of this Mannor One Tenement a water Milne and 30 acres of marsh ground lyinge at Mitcham for which he payeth the yearly rent of xxs."[23]

(The rent was a 'quit' rent, discharging the owner from manorial services.) As far as is known, Smythe had no interest in these mills other than as the landlord, and they were, presumably, let on long leases as a source of income.

The mill (which seems to have been a relatively new one, erected since 1584) together with associated property, remained in the hands of the Smythe family, as freehold tenants of the manor of Reigate, until the death of "widow Smythe". It then passed to her heirs, the Myers. George Smythe died in 1638 at the age of 67, and although he is described as of Mitcham, in the later years of his life he spent much of his time at his Mugswell Street house. His long and fascinating will, in which he detailed many valuable items of jewellery, furniture and plate, also shows that he died owning much property in Mitcham, including the *Buck's Head* at Fair Green.[6] Whereas we have no illustrations of the 'choice house' on the banks of the Wandle George had inherited, one can detect in drawings produced by Adam in 1774 the typical E-shaped ground plan of a large late 16th- or early 17th-century property.[24] The main entrance was by a doorway beneath a porch in the centre of the north elevation, giving access to the great hall which extended to the visitor's right and contained a massive chimney-piece. The kitchen and service quarters lay beyond, whilst to the left was the dining room, library and study. In his will Smythe refers to "The Great Chamber", "The Gallery", "the entry going into my closet" and "the Great Bedd whereon my Armes are embroidered at the head in Silver ... with the ffeather Bedd, Bolster and Bedclothes ...". The interior of the house certainly sounds impressive, but whether Smythe had in mind his London residence or the family home at Mitcham is not clear, although the latter seems the most likely..

By the end of the reign of James I the Smythe family's seat by the Wandle had become the residence of George's eldest son, Thomas, who in 1618 married Sarah, daughter of Sir Humphrey Handford, a merchant and alderman of the city of London.[25] In the marriage settlement the two fathers made over to the young couple in tail male the capital messuage or farm of Dunsford, and the mansion house at Mitcham. A marriage portion of £2,000 was paid by Sir Humphrey, whilst George "Smith" undertook to pay the newly-wed couple an annual allowance of £200 in quarterly instalments, to provide "diet and lodging" for Thomas and Sarah, and the same for a manservant and lady's maid, plus provisions and stabling for either two geldings or two racehorses. It was agreed that George Smith would continue to receive the rents from the estate and, in lieu of Thomas and Sarah living with him, the sum of £60 p.a.[26] These provisions seem generous indeed, and we can imagine Thomas and Sarah living very comfortably. Whether or not they resided at Mitcham Grove we cannot tell, but if Thomas had business in the city the couple would probably have kept a house in London.

One may assume that for a while all was well, but difficult times were ahead for many old-established families, and in the Civil War loyalties were frequently divided. Thomas's aunt Mary married a Sir John Leigh of Mitcham, who is described as 'a soldier', and seems to have been a high Anglican, if not actually an adherent of the 'old religion'. She lived at Hall Place, a house in Mitcham associated with recusancy since the late 16th century, and would almost certainly have sided with the King and the Royalist party.[27] Where the rest of the family's sympathies lay we cannot be sure, but Thomas, son-in-law of a prominent city merchant, seems more likely to have favoured the Parliamentary party than the Royalists. Even so, he evidently soon found himself under financial pressure and in 1645, was obliged to mortgage to John Handford of Essex, a member of the Merchant Taylors' Company and, presumably, one of his wife's relatives, much of the estate settled on him at the time of his marriage. The property was described in a 'declaration of trust' as:

"all that messuage or tenement with barns, stables and appurtenances in the occupation of Thomas Smythe
certain parcels of Marsh ground thereunto adjoining, enclosed with pales, lying in Micham containing 20 acres
certain parcels of arable ground in Carshalton commonly called Marris fee containing 40 acres
a cornmill called Micham Mill *als* Wickford Mill *als* Marrish Mill with appurtenances, and a high drying room or loft adjoining and two closes of marsh ground, all in the parish of Micham
a mill house with orchards, barns, stables, yards, outhouses and 4 acres of meadow, then in the occupation of Grace Sadler, widow
a mansion house, messuage or tenement with barns, stables, orchards, gardens and appurtenances in the occupation of Thomas Smyth
and 83 acres of land more in the occupation of Thomas Smyth"
as well as woodland in Streatham and properties in Witley.[28]

The need to raise capital evidently arose again four years later, for in 1649 Thomas and Sarah sold some 50 acres of land, including 44 acres in Marrish Fee, to Ralph Trattle, a land agent and member of the Fishmongers' Company of London.[29] Within a few years this was to form the nucleus of the estate of Robert Cranmer, an East India merchant, who purchased from Trattle the modest mansion the latter had built for himself overlooking what is now Cranmer Green.[30] A second substantial house in Lower Mitcham, occupying land once owned by the Wyche family, was sold by Thomas and Sarah to Henry Hampson, another London merchant, in 1649.[31] In the deed of sale the couple's "son" George is mentioned. We shall return to him later.

Holding office as churchwarden at Mitcham in 1653, Thomas was evidently held to be 'faithful, fearing God and hating covetousness', for he was appointed several times to act as a local assessor for the quarterly levy imposed by Cromwell to maintain the army and navy during the Protectorate.[32] With, we may imagine, interests in the city, Smith would, like many London merchants and professional men, have continued to support parliamentary government and stability, without necessarily subscribing to the views of the more radical elements and extreme Protestants. George Smith (sic), who seems to have been the grandson of George and Rosa and son of Thomas's brother William and his wife Parnell, lies buried beneath the floor of the chancel of Mitcham church, having died in October 1714 in his 80th year. His black marble ledger slab, now beneath the flooring of the south aisle, bears the arms of the family, and he is known to have inherited an estate in Mitcham on his father's death in 1640. At that time young George would have been a child of about six years of age and, as a minor, was, presumably, brought up under the guardianship of his uncle Thomas and aunt Sarah. It also appears that he may have been adopted, for, as we have seen above, he is described as Thomas's "son" in an indenture of 1649.[31] William, George's father, was styled as "of Mitcham" in 1627 when he bought the "goods, chattels and plate etc." belonging to his aunt Elizabeth Wyche of Mitcham, the widow of Richard Wyche, a London merchant who died in November 1621. Elizabeth was the daughter of George Smythe senior, and was the mother of 18 children, one of whom, Sir Peter Wyche, was "Comptroller of the house to Charles I". The circumstances of William Smythe's death are unknown, but it may be significant that 1640 was the year of the Second Bishops' War, when the Scots invaded the north of England and defeated the Royalist forces at Newburn. His uncle, Sir John Leigh, had borne arms in the king's service, and the possibility is that William Smythe, like George Carew of Beddington, was killed in the fighting around York.

Thomas Smythe died in 1658, leaving debts to George who by this time had reached manhood. Whatever their allegiances, on the Restoration the social standing of the Smythe family seems to have emerged unimpaired. Having come of age, George Smythe, or Smith, as the name is more commonly rendered by this time, had become the owner of the house by the waterside at Mitcham in about 1655, and was already one of the leading residents in the village when, in 1663/4, he was assessed for tax on the basis of 14 hearths.[33] If these were all under one roof, it can be taken as an indication that his was a house of considerable size, and without doubt one of the largest in the parish. It also had innovations, and in a letter written to John Aubrey in 1675/6 John Evelyn, having described a 'Smokejack' installed in the kitchen chimney at his brother's house at Wotton, commented that "Mr. Smith of Micham's Spits are turn'd by the Water, which indeed runs thro' his House". The "water" he referred to as "the most Chrystal Stream we have in our Country, and comes from Beddington".[34] Evelyn was obviously alluding to the Wandle, but it was unlikely to have been the river itself that ran through Smith's house, but rather a leat taken from upstream. At the Quarter Sessions at Reigate in April 1663 "George Smith of Mitcham esquire" was appointed treasurer for the East and Middle Divisions of Surrey for moneys to be collected for "the relief of maimed soldiers, gaols, hospitals and poor prisoners in the King's Bench and Marshalsea prisons".[35] His response to the court's commission seems to have fallen short of his obligations for, at the quarter sessions at Guildford in 1667 he was indicted for having refused to execute the order of the Reigate court, and was ordered to do so within three weeks or face a fine of £50. As is so often the case, the records are silent on the outcome. We are left to assume that Smith complied, and can only speculate on the reasons for his apparent disobedience. Could his contempt of the court be seen as an expression of disaffection with, or even defiance of, the Cavalier Parliament of Charles II and the administration of Clarendon?

In 1669 George Smith, styled "of Wandsworth", granted a 21-year lease of the *Buck's Head* inn, overlooking the Upper Green, and 21 acres of land in Mitcham to a Matthew Bowman.[36] Two years later, in June 1671, he mortgaged Dunsford farm and Garretts farm, with appurtenances, to Ambrose Phillips and son for £1,000 and payment of £1,060 "voids". By concurrent deed poll the Phillipses affirmed that they were acting as trustees for Anthony Keck esq, who provided the money, and the following February, £1,035 having been paid to them and £465 to George Smith, the property was assigned to Keck. Interest charges were met and part of the principal had been repaid by 1678, when Smith decided to sell both properties.

Nothing more seems to have been recorded of George Smith's activities, and it has not been ascertained if he married. A survey of the manor of Reigate in 1700 noted the claim of a "widow Smith" to the freehold tenure of one "Messuage or Tenement with a Water Mill now used for the working of copper and a parcel of Marsh ground there unto belonging situate and being at Mitcham, Conteining 30 acres" for which she paid 20 shillings per annum, but in the absence of a christian name one cannot identify her with certainty.[37] The Smith family's influence in Mitcham affairs remained throughout the early 18th century, the vestry book for 1699, for instance, showing that a Thomas Smith senior and his son Thomas were appointed members of the then newly formed select vestry, a self-perpetuating body of local landed proprietors concerned with parochial administration. Thomas Smith (presumably the son) continued to serve as a vestryman until around 1736.

The Myers Family (1715–1742)

Through the medium of the court rolls of Reigate,[38] tenure of the mill and the land associated with it and, by implication, ownership of the Mitcham Grove estate, can be traced from the Smiths or Smythes to the Myers, another family of local importance to whom they were related by marriage. Mrs Smith and "Mr. Miers and his wife" were listed amongst the 'Gentry &c.' of the parish by the vicar, William Hatsell, in the answers he gave to the bishop of Winchester's visitation of 1725[39] and we find William Myers of King Street, London, being admitted to the tenancy of the manor in 1726, having inherited the estate the previous year from his kinswoman Susannah Smythe.[40] (Will: Appendix 1a) William's precise relationship is not clear, but Susannah, who was described as a spinster, could have been George Smith's unmarried sister, and William's aunt. Myers in his turn bequeathed the estate to his eldest son on his death in 1742.[41] (Will: Appendix 1b)

In 1715, following the death of George Smith, who held various parcels of land in Mitcham as a customary tenant, the court rolls of the manor of Biggin and Tamworth record the admission of William Myers, then of Watling Street, London and described as an attorney, to the tenancy of that manor.[42] The date he took over the family house is not known,

but the vicar's inclusion of William amongst the gentry of the parish in
1725 suggests the Myers family may already have been resident at
Mitcham Grove before Susannah Smythe's death.

Whereas we have no illustrations or contemporary descriptions of the
house William Myers inherited in 1726, the plan prepared by Robert
Adam in 1774, when extensions were under consideration, shows that
at the core of the 18th-century building was a house typical of the late
Elizabethan period. The front entrance, on the north-east elevation, either
side of which were projecting wings, opened directly into the hall, 38
feet long by 20 feet wide and extended to the right. In sale particulars
produced in 1828 there is mention of an "ancient arched stone chimney
piece", which had clearly once occupied a central position on the far
wall of the hall, behind which was an inner hall containing a "handsome

Mitcham Grove – southern elevation – watercolour c.1830
reproduced by courtesy of Merton Library & Heritage Service

oak staircase with balusters and gallery". Both dining and drawing rooms are said to have had "statuary marble chimneypieces", and it is not difficult to imagine the general appearance of the interior, no doubt similar in many respects to numerous examples which still survive, both in Surrey and further afield. Later engravings and paintings of Mitcham Grove show signs of its having been transformed externally in the late 17th or early 18th century with the installation of boxed sash windows, the addition of a classical pediment on the south-west front and, running all round the building, a heavily modillioned cornice topped with a parapet wall and balustrading.

There is no firm evidence that William Myers and his family used Mitcham Grove as their country home in the late 1720s and '30s, but the signs are that they did and, moreover, that they took their expected place in local society. This impression is supported by the fact that the two premier families in the village were united in 1743 by the marriage of 30-year-old William Myers junior, an arts graduate of Lincoln College, Oxford,[43] to Elizabeth Cranmer,[44] daughter of James Cranmer, the squire of Mitcham.

With the death of William Myers senior in 1742 the story of Mitcham Grove seems to have entered a new phase. As far as we can tell no longer the seat of one of Mitcham's oldest families, it was leased for the next quarter century or so to a succession of tenants whose involvement in national affairs was by no means insignificant, and was then sold. Meanwhile, William and Elizabeth Myers were living in what later became known as the 'Manor House', a largely 18th-century residence off London Road, Lower Mitcham, just to the south of the Cricket Green. The *Alumni Oxonienses*, recording the matriculation at the age of 19 of yet another William Myers, this time at Pembroke College in 1763, describes the father as "of Mitcham", and entitled to bear arms. William and Elizabeth's third son, the Reverend Streynsham Derbyshire Myers MA of Magdalen College, Oxford, was appointed to the living at Mitcham under the patronage of his uncle James Cranmer in 1779, and remained the incumbent until his death in 1824.

Scots at Mitcham Grove (1755–1786)

Archibald Stewart and Alexander Wedderburn

The oldest surviving poor rate book for the parish of Mitcham is for September 1755,[45] and lists Archibald Stewart (to be misspelt by the overseers as "Steward" or "Stuart" over the next 18 years) as the 'proprietor' and occupier of Mitcham Grove. In all probability he held the property on a lease from Myers, and an apparent break in the continuity of his occupation may perhaps be explained by the granting of a sub-lease to a Robert Paulk, whose name appears in the rate books for a couple of years in the late '60s.

Boswell, in his *London Journal*, recorded his meeting with Stewart, "formerly the noted Provost at Edinburgh" at a dinner party of "half-English gentry" in London in May 1763. Stewart had been provost in 1745 and, according to Professor F A Pottle, "opposed all plans for arming the city, so that the Highland army entered without opposition. After the collapse of the Rebellion he was arrested and put in the Tower (he was MP for Edinburgh), and in 1747 was tried before the High Court of Judiciary for neglect of duty and misbehaviour in the execution of his office. The verdict (a popular one) was not guilty".[46]

By 1759 Stewart's son John[47] had become a partner in the family wine business, and was also connected with the East India Company. According to Valentine,[48] John Stewart was an aide and supporter of Clive, and in 1766 became assistant to Sir George Colebrook. He was elected member of parliament for Arundel in 1771, representing that constituency until 1774. Throughout this time he supported Colebrook's interests, though there is no record that he ever addressed the House of Commons. The younger Stewart is described by Valentine as "of Mitcham",[49] but his connection with the village seems to have been severed in the summer of 1773 when his father's name ceases to appear in the rate books. At about this time John Stewart commenced writing and publishing articles on East India Company affairs. Two years later he was in financial straits, and took no further part in politics.

In March 1764 Archibald Stewart and William Myers II were joint signatories of a lease conveying to Robert Cochran, a surgeon and apothecary of Mitcham, the 'millhouse and three water corn mills therein' (i.e. three mills in one building) and several parcels of land lying upstream from Mitcham bridge most, if not all, of which had been part of the Smythe estate since the 16th century.[50] Through the medium of the steadily increasing volume of local records the subsequent history of this triple mill can be followed throughout the rest of the 18th and 19th centuries. As the Grove mill, rebuilt many times but on more or less its original site, it still stands, although no longer a mill, having been converted to flats. The site of another, separate, mill the former Crown mill, was incorporated in a housing development in 2004. The 18th-century miller's house survives, and is now one of a group of three picturesque pantiled and weatherboarded houses overlooking the river.

According to notes deposited in Mitcham library by Miss Farewell Jones, a local historian in the 1930s, William Myers, "an attorney of London" and heir to the Smythe estate, sold the Mitcham Grove estate to Lord Clive.[51] Unfortunately, Miss Jones, the daughter of a local solicitor and a generally reliable authority, did not quote the source of this vital scrap of information, but she may have had access to an abstract of title. The precise date of the transaction thus remains unknown. In 1769 Clive, recently returned from India, purchased the Duke of Newcastle's estate at Claremont, near Esher. He is said to have found Claremont inconvenient, but there is no record of his having resided at Mitcham. A new Claremont House was under construction to the designs of Launcelot ('Capability') Brown and Henry Holland when Clive died in 1774.[52]

Regrettably, not all the early Mitcham poor rate books survive, otherwise the gap in our knowledge might be closed. However, the book for September 1773 shows that by then the Mitcham Grove estate had become the property of Alexander Wedderburn, and from this point on the history of the house is clear. Sir John Soane's Museum possesses two sets of plans and elevations produced by Robert Adam for Wedderburn in October 1774.[53] Both schemes incorporate as a common element what was evidently the existing house, which would seem to have come into Wedderburn's possession the previous year. (Soane, it is perhaps worth observing, worked on Claremont under Brown and Holland in 1772, when only 19.)

1st Baron Clive, 1725-74
from the picture by Dance, engraved in Malcolm's Life of Clive
and reproduced in C Macfarlane and T Thomson
The Comprehensive History of England *III (1877) p693*

In the more ambitious of his two proposals, Adam suggested to his client an impressive remodelling which, whilst retaining much of the original building, would have transformed it into an elegantly proportioned mansion in the fashionable classical idiom for which the architect is famous. To the north-east, south-east and south-west fronts he proposed the addition of colonnades. The existing doorcase and main entrance door on the north-eastern side of the house were to be removed, and in their stead Adam designed a most imposing entrance from the north-west. Here a pediment supported by four Doric columns was envisaged

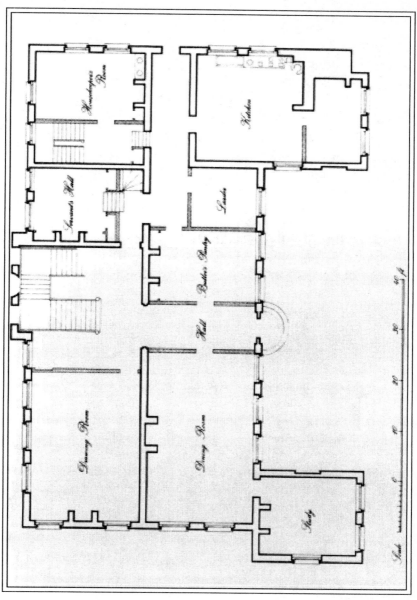

*Copy, by Norman Plastow, of Robert Adam's Plan of Mitcham
Grove in 1774, now in Sir John Soane's Museum*

towering above the new doorway, which was to be approached from a gravelled court flanked on either side by new domestic wings built in the Palladian style. Internally, Adam suggested further drastic alterations, the former domestic offices giving way to a new double-apsed entrance hall 30 feet long by 22 feet deep, and an "eating room" 36 feet by 20. In the south wing he proposed retention of the drawing room and study, but added an antechamber giving onto a colonnade with views of the west lawn and river.

The second of Adam's schemes was far more conservative, retaining much of the original structure, including the seven fireplaces on the ground floor which, with the corresponding seven on the upper storey, tally neatly with the 14 on which George Smith had paid hearth tax a century earlier. For reasons on which one can only speculate, the second scheme seems to have been that which Wedderburn favoured, although he adopted several of the features from Adam's more extravagant alternative. One of these, a semi-circular loggia on the north-west front, can be seen clearly in drawings of Mitcham Grove in Henry Hoare's time. We may also ascribe to this period the building of a two-storeyed extension on the south-western corner of the house, balancing the small projecting wing containing the study.

Adam's ground floor plan of Mitcham Grove, confirmed in part by the excavations conducted by Surrey Archaeological Society in 1974, shows that the house was of quite modest proportions for a gentleman's residence of the late 18th century. The drawing room, dining room and study lay to the left of the former hall, by this time subdivided to provide a butler's pantry and larder, and the domestic quarters were situated to the right, in the north wing. At the rear the principal staircase led, via a half-landing, to the first floor, passing large windows overlooking the lawn and the river. The unchanging assessments for poor rate and land tax are indications that the house was not enlarged significantly during Wedderburn's ownership, and in fact its external appearance changed comparatively little in the years following his departure from Mitcham, although Henry Hoare is alleged to have developed the grounds very considerably after purchase in 1786, adding an approach courtyard and "other refinements"[54] which probably included the castelled entrance lodges. The sale particulars surviving from 1828 certainly indicate that when auctioned by Henry Hoare's executors the house was essentially the same "spendid villa" with which Clive was to reward Wedderburn for his legal services so handsomely in 1773.

Much of the biographical content of what follows, dealing with Alexander Wedderburn, Henry Hoare and Sir John Lubbock, was compiled between 1970 and 1973 by the late Doris M Dawes, a fellow member of Merton Historical Society. Out of respect for her scholarship, and in acknowledgement of her considerable contribution to our knowledge of these three very great men, her notes are reproduced with the minimum of alteration, and with only a few additions.[55]

Alexander Wedderburn, though not greatly involved in parish affairs during his residence in Mitcham, deserves a place in local history in recognition of his achievements in a wider sphere. Born in Edinburgh in February 1733, he studied law and, being extremely ambitious, settled in England in 1757 having decided the English bar would offer him far greater opportunities for advancement than that of Scotland. He was proved correct, for in 1760, through the influence of Lord Bute, his intimate friend, he became member of Parliament for the Ayr burghs, and by 1763 a King's Counsel. Like Boswell, who found him overbearing and flippant, many people disliked his conceit and resented his success. In 1771 Wedderburn secured the post of Solicitor General, in which office he was described as "acute, perspicacious, elegant and persuasive" and to have "alternatively essayed the force of reason and the charms of eloquence; sometimes attacking the judgement with refined argument; at other times appealing to the fancy with the powers of wit and graces of elocution".

With these attributes it is little wonder that Wedderburn's ambitions were realised, although his political life was not particularly savoury. Whereas he entered Parliament as a Tory, he showed no scruples in changing his views should this be to his advantage, shifting his ground first to support the Radical, John Wilkes, and then, to gain the post of Solicitor General, he became a Whig. This last manoeuvre has been described as "One of the most flagrant cases of ratting recorded in our party annals". Wedderburn's marriage to an heiress in 1767 brought him a considerable fortune, which helped him to indulge his liking for splendour; he later claimed that on the day he became Solicitor General he had ordered a service of plate which cost him £8,000. He had, however, another side to his nature, for in 1771 it was mainly he who obtained a government pension for Dr Johnson, who was then in need, defending the grant when this was queried by a member of Parliament with the retort that "the Dictionary of the English Language was reason enough for public bounty".

In the House of Commons in May 1773 Wedderburn conducted a masterly defence of Lord Clive, who was faced with a motion charging him with abuse of the powers entrusted to him in India, and of amassing a private fortune of £250,000. In an all-night sitting Wedderburn persuaded members to reject the censure motion with an amendment that Clive's career had brought great credit on himself and his country. Clive rewarded his defender not only with money but also with the gift of a "spendid villa and estate in Mitcham in Surrey". This was, of course, Mitcham Grove, which in Wedderburn's possession became the centre of a busy social life. "Here he used on Saturdays and Sundays to entertain the great and witty. He likewise had an elegant house in Lincolns Inn Fields; in horses and equipage he rivalled the nobility." Through his wife he possessed an estate in Yorkshire, and he liked to go there at times and act the country squire.

By June 1778 Wedderburn had become Attorney General, in which position he assisted in the first relaxation of the Roman Catholic penal code in Ireland. Then, in 1779, came the threat of invasion by France and Spain. On the grounds that shortages of men were such that six or eight ships of the line at Portsmouth were useless for want of crews, Wedderburn introduced a bill for unrestricted impressment into the service. The measure was rushed through Parliament, and became law on the third day.

Wedderburn's next advance came the following year, when he became Lord Chief Justice to the Court of Common Pleas, and was raised to the peerage as Lord Loughborough of Loughborough in the County of Leicester; he had also become friendly with the Prince of Wales, and was often called upon for advice by the Prince during George III's illness. For another six years he continued to live at Mitcham Grove; then in April 1786 he sold the house and estate to Henry Hoare. Wedderburn reached the peak of his career in 1798 when he achieved his ambition of becoming Lord Chancellor, a position he was to retain until his resignation in 1801, when he was created Earl Rosslyn and retired to his villa near Windsor. On 31 December 1804 he was present at a royal party at Frogmore, apparently in his usual good health. The following day he collapsed and died. He was buried in St Paul's Cathedral.

There are two entries in the Mitcham vestry minutes recording occasions when Wedderburn's help was requested in connection with local matters. In 1780 – the year he became Lord Chief Justice – the churchwardens and overseers were considering the erection of a new workhouse, and decided to ask the great man's assistance in obtaining Parliamentary sanction. They were advised that this was unnecessary, and proceeded with the erection of a workhouse on the Common in 1782 at a cost of £1,200. The second occasion was in 1783, when there was a dispute concerning the payment of poor rates, several persons having refused to pay a rate computed on the gross rent, i.e. including that portion of the inclusive rent which was to meet the land tax demanded of the landowner. One objector declared that he would abide by Lord Loughborough's decision, and the parish's most distinguished resident was accordingly asked to give his opinion. His answer was that as the land tax was part of the rent it was therefore liable to poor rate. Upon which, presumably, the objectors paid up.

Henry Hoare of Mitcham (1786–1828)

The purchase of Mitcham Grove (for the sum of £18,000) by Henry Hoare inaugurated a very different era both at the house and in the village, for it would seem impossible to imagine a greater contrast between two men than that between Lord Loughborough and the new owner. The former, an ambitious stateman, childless, fond of display and with little time to give to local concerns and, the latter a banker, happily married with five children, who, almost at once, took his place as a leader in the community.

The banking firm of Henry Hoare and Company, of which Henry Hoare was a member, had been founded by his great-grandfather Sir Richard Hoare who, the grandson of a Buckinghamshire yeoman farmer, had been apprenticed at the age of 17 to the trade of goldsmith. By 1672 he had established his own business as a goldsmith and banker in Cheapside 'at the sign of the Golden Bottle'. In 1690 the business was transferred to the site of the present bank, C Hoare & Co, at 37 Fleet Street, EC4, where a gilded leather bottle is still displayed. Not long after Sir Richard's death the business became confined to banking. Neither Henry Hoare's father nor his grandfather were connected with the firm, and his entry into it had brought back the senior branch of the family.

Henry being a name which occurs often in the Hoare family, it became necessary to employ nicknames in order to distinguish them; hence 'Fat Henry', 'Magnificent Henry', and 'Henry of Mitcham'. The latter, born in 1750 and educated at Eton, was already a partner in the bank when he came to Mitcham Grove. A year later, in 1787, he became senior partner, a position he was to hold until his death in 1828, although towards the end of his life he directed the business from his home at Mitcham. Extremely able and industrious, he is remembered in the bank today for the success with which he guided the business through 40 years of unprecedented anxiety and difficulty. Never before had the banking system of this country been faced with problems of such complexity, for to the fiscal effects of the growing momentum of the Industrial Revolution were added the alarm and uncertainty engendered by the French Revolution and the inflationary influence of the Napoleonic Wars. Peace brought no respite, and to the trials of post-war depression and unemployment were added the stresses imposed by the continuing process of change in British industrial organisation and the introduction of new manufacturing techniques.

In February 1775 Henry Hoare had married Lydia Henrietta Malortie, the daughter and co-heiress of Isaac Malortie, a merchant of Hanover and London, and when they came to Mitcham Grove they already had five children: four sons and a daughter. Active in his support of important church and charitable societies, Henry Hoare very soon added to these interests those of Mitcham. During the next 40 years little business of

Henry Hoare
reproduced by courtesy of Merton Library & Heritage Service

any importance to the village was discussed or transacted without his assistance, and the firm signature of 'Henry Hoare' appears throughout the parish vestry minutes. From reading these one is left in no doubt that he must have been an outstanding member of the vestry, always ready to undertake whatever was asked of him, and a regular attender of meetings. Mention of some of his interests will show something, though only a little, of their number and variety.

Perhaps what proved to be one of the biggest and longest of his local commitments commenced in 1789 when he became one of the six members of a committee appointed to be responsible for the building of the gallery and other alterations to the parish church. For years the condition of the ancient building had been a matter of concern, and for the next quarter of a century opinions veered continuously between enlarging and repairing on the one hand, and complete rebuilding on the other.[56] Henry Hoare continued to serve on the committee throughout the war, and when in 1819 it was finally decided to demolish and rebuild the church, he not only became treasurer of the rebuilding fund, but also lent a large sum of money. From then until 1827, the year before he died, he presented the rebuilding account each year to the Easter vestry. Some indication of Henry Hoare's continuing generosity to the church is given in the story recounted by Robert Masters Chart, whose grandfather, John Chart, was the builder of the new church under the direction of George Smith, the architect. It appears that Henry Hoare, a churchwarden, when taking the collections at the church doors, was "in the habit of placing in his plate a five pound note and five sovereigns – the latter, he said, to keep the note from blowing away".[57] After nearly two centuries of devaluation such a donation would still be exceptional; in those days it must have represented a fortune.

In the spring of 1791 Henry Hoare was appointed a justice of the peace for the county, and also one of the two overseers of the poor for the parish of Mitcham. Shortly after his appointment to the latter office it was reported that the workhouse children needed further assistance in reading tuition than the master of the workhouse was capable of giving them. Henry Hoare's influence is not difficult to detect in the unanimous decision of the vestry that a teacher should be employed on Thursday,

Saturday and Sunday afternoons "for instructing the children in reading and saying their catechism" at a wage of three shillings per week. This arrangement continued for almost three years, and then, a women having entered the workhouse who was considered capable of taking over the instruction, an opportunity for economy occurred and the teacher was dismissed.

At the end of the 18th century the revolution in France and the subsequent outbreak of hostilities with Britain led to a very real fear of French invasion. Patriotic fervour swept the country, and on all sides preparations were made for defence, not least in Mitcham where the alarmed vestry met to "fix on a plan to defend this parish from the enemy". Needless to say, the first step taken was to appoint a committee to deal with the problem, and Henry Hoare was of course among its members. Very soon plans were made for the formation of an 'Armed Association', to consist of two corps, one of cavalry and another of infantry "armed and accoutred at their own expense", whilst those unable to learn the use of arms were to provide themselves with ten-foot long pikes or constables' staves. It was stressed that these arrangements "were for the sole purpose of protecting their own property and for the Peace and Tranquility of this Parish on the occasion of Invasion, Rebellion, Insurrection, Civil Commotions or other cases of Extra-ordinary Emergency ... and Ladies and Gentlemen and other respectable inhabitants of the said Parish" were to be asked to contribute in aid of the association. Many readers will recall how history was repeated during the Second World War when appeals were made for those not already in the armed forces to train for local defence, and the men of Mitcham once more formed themselves into volunteer companies of what later became the Home Guard. "Bring any weapon" was the order, and in the early summer of 1940 men armed with clubs, staves and, in one case, a cavalry sword turned out and drilled on Mitcham Common.

Never one for a passive role, Henry Hoare threw himself into the preparations and was soon deeply committed. Hannah More, a visitor to Mitcham Grove in 1798, recorded in her diary for 17 May: "I did not enjoy much of poor Mr. Hoare's company, so occupied was he in arming and exercising. He rises at half-past four at Mitcham, trots off to town to be ready to meet at six the Fleet Street Corps, performing their evolutions in the area of Bridewell, the only place where they can find sufficient space; then comes back to a late dinner, and as soon as it is over goes to his committees, after which he has a sergeant to drill himself and his three sons on the lawn until it is dark."[58] When it is remembered that as senior partner Henry Hoare was at this time charged with the exacting task of guiding the family bank through a very troubled period in the financial world and of making far-reaching decisions, this evidence of his whole-hearted involvement in national and local affairs emphasises the strong sense of duty which pervaded his life. One feels the resolve and stamina of lesser mortals would have been sapped by the sheer effort of daily commuting betwen Mitcham and Fleet Street over the roads of the time.

The need to educate the country's poorer children led to the foundation of the National Schools Society by the Church of England in 1811 and 'National' or Church Schools built by voluntary subscriptions gradually became a feature of towns and villages throughout the country. Encouraged by Henry Hoare, the Mitcham vestry resolved that it should follow the national trend, and decided upon an extension to the existing Sunday School premises, the whole building to be capable of holding 200 children. Now grimy with age, the schools building is still to be seen on Lower Green West, and above the entrance door an inscribed tablet dated 1812 bears Henry Hoare's name as Treasurer.

The parish vestry certainly had good cause to note in its minutes, as it often did, thanks for the help so willingly given by this member, one of these entries being made on the occasion of his having a cottage built at the workhouse for the accommodation of the sick. The gratitude felt by the villagers is expressed in the minute of 2 April 1793, which records "... that the thanks of parish in Vestry assembled be given to Henry Hoare Esq, for his kindness in Erecting and furnishing a Cottage at his own Expence by the Side of the Workhouse for the use of poor people afflicted with any Infectious Disorders that might be pernicious to the poor in the House; and it is likewise ordered that the Vestry Clerk do transcribe the last order of Vestry and wait upon Henry Hoare Esq.

with the same". Until 1973 the cottage stood fronting Windmill Road, surrounded on three sides by the factory of S & R J Everett Co Ltd. It was the sole remaining building from the workhouse complex, and at the time of its demolition few Mitcham people were aware of the compassionate and generous impulse to which it owed its origin.

The education of the poorer members of the parish made further progress in 1816 when the vestry agreed that the schools building should be used for an evening school established for adults and others unable to obtain instruction during the day. Thus it was that the first 'Adult Education Classes' were started in Mitcham nearly 200 years ago. Consideration of further means of helping this section of the village population to help themselves led to the formation of the Mitcham Savings Bank in 1819, a project with which another member of the Hoare family came forward to assist, in the person of George Matthew Hoare, Henry's third son. George became treasurer whilst his father held the office of president, and with these two at the helm, the bank proved a most successful venture, the number of depositors steadily increasing until by 1825 it reported over 300, ten of whom had deposits of between £100 and £150. Henry Hoare retained the presidency until his death, upon which his son took his place.[59]

With so many interests, it is perhaps not surprising that in one of his roles, that of a gentleman farmer, Henry Hoare should have fallen short of the standards of his day. In 1786 he had purchased from Lord Loughborough two farms to the south of Mitcham on the clay lands rising to Rose Hill. Known as Batt's Farm and Pig or Hill Farm, they lay in Carshalton parish between Wrythe Lane and the London to Sutton turnpike. James Malcolm, compiling his *Compendium of Modern Husbandry* published in 1806, said of these two farms, by then run as one unit of considerable extent.

> "... the land is strong and holding, but in the course of my frequent observations on the state of the husbandry pursued thereon, I never saw anything to commend. Were I to pass my opinion on the cause, it would be something like this, that the master, unless he takes great pride in seeing that the business of his farm is well managed, and in leaving it altogether to the management of a

bailiff, unless he be one of those rarities which we now and then meet with, is not likely to have things conducted in the best style. As a merchant or banker he may have something else to do, besides watching the actions of his servant, and being ignorant of the profession, he is at a loss to commend, when to disapprove, or when to recommend a different mode of proceeding; and if his bailiff, after paying all the charges, brings him something more than £5 percent on his capital, he thinks himself well satisfied, forgetting, perhaps, if he had rent to pay, and a part of that capital to repay at some future time, that it would be a losing concern.

"The land is far from being clean, nor is it well ploughed, nor early enough for soil that is so tenacious; the ditches are choked up at every other time, but when a new hedge or ditch is made, and then it is too contracted; the hedges are besides in bad order for a gentleman farmer; and those mixens [dunghills] which we see by the roadside are not made with skill or science.

"I should be sorry if what I have just advanced should do the man an injury, because he is an utter stranger to me; I had much rather in detailing his routine, have had a great deal to have commended. The crops are moderately good, certainly not what they might be so near the London dunghills."[60]

With all Henry Hoare's work and interests – of which the foregoing are only a small part – the home life at Mitcham Grove was not neglected, and as the children grew up and married their old home remained the centre to which they, and in due course their children, constantly returned. The eldest son, William Henry Hoare,[61] entered the family bank, and became a partner in 1798. On his marriage to the Hon. Louise Elizabeth Noel the young couple settled at Broomfield, Clapham, which for ten years from 1797 until 1807 had been the home of the great William Wilberforce, the slavery abolitionist. Here the Hoares were drawn into the Evangelical 'Clapham Sect', numbering amongst their friends the Macaulays, Hannah More, and Henry Thornton.[62] When their eldest son was born in December 1807, William Wilberforce himself was the baby's godfather. Bereavement came to Henry Hoare in 1816 when his wife Lydia died at the age of 62, and this year also saw the death of his daughter-in-law Louise, followed three years later by the death of William Henry. Their six young children – three sons and three daughters – were then taken, together with their governess, to live with their grandfather at Mitcham Grove. A description of the house at the time of the children's arrival provides a picture of what must have been a truly happy home

> "... Mitcham Grove was a little world in itself. And while it rivalled any house in England in comfort and ease, there was a regularity and refinement about it which did a boy good. Surrounded with pleasant lawns and gardens and a clear silvery trout stream, it was by turns the resort of all the various branches of the family, who looked upon Mr. Hoare as their head. A well-stocked library was one of the great attractions of the place ... It was the habit of Mr. Hoare to attend on Sundays to the catechizing of his grandchildren; and also on weekdays to give some further portion of his valuable time to the revising of the holiday task ... He would not infrequently make his elder grandson his companion at his early breakfast table, where he would talk to him privately on many subjects."

One of the stories told to his grandson was that when he was at Eton with Rowland Hill, they were made the sport of boys for saying their prayers before going to bed, receiving a shower of pins in their feet. This boy, another Henry, was his grandfather's heir. Great care was taken with his upbringing; and after Eton and Cambridge – where he took his degree at the age of 19 – he entered the bank.

In 1822 another member of Henry Hoare's family died; his second son Henry Villars Hoare, born in 1777, who died unmarried at Mitcham Grove. The third son, George Matthew Hoare (1779-1852) became a brewer, his father having purchased the Red Lion Brewery (later to be known as Hoare & Co Ltd) in 1802 and placed him in it. George married Angeline Frances Greene, daughter and co-heiress of a Lancashire landowner, in October 1810 at Morden parish church (his younger brother Charles James officiating) and afterwards lived at The Lodge, Morden, from whence he was active in both Morden and Mitcham. High infantile mortality was common at this time amongst rich and poor alike, and a tablet in the church records the death in infancy of six of their children. The census returns of 1851 show George Matthew Hoare, widower of 71, magistrate and landowner, still living at The Lodge, Morden, together with his son, daughter-in-law and three grandchildren, farming 250 acres. Eleven servants were employed including two footmen, a butler and a coachman, and 12 men worked on the farm. A window in the south wall of Morden parish church commemorates George Matthew and his wife, who died in 1846.

After obtaining several honours at St John's College, Cambridge (of which he was later a fellow), Charles James Hoare (1781-1865), Henry Hoare's youngest son, entered the Church, being ordained in 1804. He was married in July 1811 to Jane Isabella Holden of Mitcham, amongst the signatures in the parish register being that of William Wilberforce, and in 1821 he became rector of Godstone, his father being patron of the living. He subsequently became rural dean of Ewell, archdeacon of Winchester and in 1847 of Surrey.[63] Charles Hoare's arrival at Godstone began a lengthy connection of the family with the parish, as from that time onwards until 1930, and then again from 1955 until 1965, the rectory was in their hands. Henry Gerard Hoare of Stansted, who died in 1896, was churchwarden for almost 40 years. A century later the family was still represented in the parish.

The Mitcham registers record that Charles also officiated on 7 April 1808 at the marriage of his only sister, Lydia Elizabeth (1786-1856) to Sir Thomas Dyke Acland of Killerton in the county of Devon. Sir Thomas (1787-1871), the tenth baronet, took his bride to the family seat at Killerton House, seven miles north-east of Exeter. Here one can still see a chamber organ built in 1807 for Lydia, on which she had lessons from Samuel Wesley (grandson of Charles) who was organist at Exeter Cathedral. The house and beautiful grounds (now National Trust property) are still very much as they were in Sir Thomas's time. There is a romantic story of Sir Thomas proposing to Lydia in the summerhouse at Mitcham Grove, and a replica of this little building was erected on the Aclands' Holnicote estate in Somerset. Like the rest of the family, the Aclands (they had nine children) were to continue to find happiness when visiting Mitcham, and when Henry Hoare died Sir Thomas had a memorial tablet placed immediately above the pew in the parish church of St Peter and St Paul where Henry regularly worshipped for 40 years. A bound volume of sketches of Mitcham by Sir Thomas, dated 1828 and presumably made at around the time of Henry Hoare's death, is in the possession of the Acland family.[64]

Henry Hoare's life came to an end in March 1828. During his long residence in Mitcham he had fully and successfully taken his part in so much that concerned the village community, had been the centre of a happy family life which also embraced a wide circle of friends, and had in addition occupied with distinction the most responsible position in Hoare's Bank. He was buried in the family grave in Morden churchyard, and a white marble tablet to the west of the pulpit commemorates him, his wife, two sons and several grandchildren. Another memorial, erected by his grandson, is in the church at Staplehurst, Kent, where he held another estate.

As might be expected, Henry Hoare's will, a document of seven closely written pages, is of considerable interest, although much of it, dealing with the disposal of his bonds and other securities, is of no direct concern to the local historian. (Appendix 1c) His grandson was left an extensive estate, but did not inherit Mitcham Grove. This, together with land and buildings in Mitcham, Morden, Carshalton, Sutton and elsewhere in Surrey, was left to his sons George and Charles and two other Hoares, with instructions that it should all be sold either by public auction or private contracts, and the money used in accordance with his directions. There were many bequests in the will, such as £100 to Mitcham Sunday School, and £40 to Richard Cranmer, vicar of Mitcham; no-one seems to have been forgotten, least of all the servants at Mitcham Grove. One bequest is particularly striking, illustrating the compassion with which Henry Hoare had always regarded the poor of the parish; in it he directed that William Giles (presumably his steward or bailiff) was to pay out £12 per week for the first four weeks after his master's death to poor persons "as has been usually done by him". Clearly, for some time past this sum had been distributed regularly from Mitcham Grove, apart from other benefactions. Its termination must have been a tragedy for its recipients.

Mitcham Grove – a Description

When offered for sale in 1828 the Mitcham Grove estate, of 620 acres, extended across the turnpike road to Sutton and included the grounds of Mitcham Hall, to be developed many years later as Mitcham Park. It also embraced the Watermeads and the Grove mills, Poulter Park and farmland in Carshalton parish extending as far south as Rose Hill, and much of the Ravensbury estate to the south of the Wandle in the parish of Morden.[65] Fortunately the appearance of the house in the early 19th century was preserved for posterity, and numerous engravings, sketches and watercolour drawings from the early years of the 19th century survive in the collections of public libraries and record offices. With artistic licence the detail and consequently the accuracy of the portrayal varies, but a common element is the impression of restrained good taste and an enchanting setting. In some respects the house showed the influence of Palladio as interpreted by Inigo Jones; neo-classical details had been used with discernment, and the overall effect was one of excellent proportion and balance. To date an existing house precisely is often difficult enough, and even greater uncertainty must attend an attempt based solely on drawings. One can say, however, that behind Mitcham Grove's mid-18th-century exterior with its early 19th-century modifications, the house could well have dated from the late 16th or early 17th centuries, a theory which is supported by the evidence from the excavations conducted on the site in 1974.

Part of the red brick boundary wall of Mitcham Grove survives abutting the road north from Mitcham bridge. Long gone are the castellated Gothic lodges, probably of late 18th-century date, which in the 1820s stood either side of the double gates barring entry from the turnpike road. Beyond, a gravelled drive wound round an extensive shrubbery to terminate in a sweep in front of the house, where beneath a columned portico folding glazed doors opened into the outer entrance hall. In plan the house formed a half-H, its central portion of seven bays being flanked by two wings of unequal size projecting towards the north-east. It was of three storeys throughout, the attic dormers protruding through the hipped, tiled roof. Stucco covered the external walls, the plainness of which was relieved by louvred window shutters, a bold string course at first floor level, and a modillioned cornice beneath a parapet wall pierced by sections of balustrading. The south-western facade, overlooking the river, was a little more impressive, and incorporated a centrally positioned pediment above a semi-circular columned loggia. The sale particulars of 1828 evoke images of gracious rooms inside and the reference to "an Ancient arched Stone Chimneypiece" in the butler's pantry, which had been created by a subdivision of the original hall, is an indication that an earlier building was encapsulated within successive extensions and modifications.

It is understandable that this beautiful house and its grounds should have attracted the attention of artists, topographical writers and historians, none of whom conveyed their impressions with greater eloquence than Hassell, who wrote in 1817

> "... We now return to the Wandle, which, after leaving the snuff-mill on the left of the road, passes by an arched way into the grounds of Mr. Hoare; where its first entrance is obscured by an immense quantity of high trees, forming the commencement of the Grove. Leaving this recess, in a serpentine form, the larger body of the stream takes a course to the left, within a short distance of the house. A smaller stream resembling a canal, is conducted on the right side of the mansion; where it turns a wheel, by which the water is conveyed in pipes to every part of the house that requires it; it also supplies the outhouses and dairy, which is a pretty rustic building, and is thatched, and partly obscured from the site by an immense quantity of timber that surrounds the villa. The hot and green-houses, and the pleasure gardens are on the right side of this small canal; which, after coursing the pleasure-grounds for some distance, joins the stream at the furthest extremity of the grove.

> "The main stream is the principal ornament to the grounds, which are particularly beautified by immense groups of large trees, the accompaniment of its banks, obscuring its waters at certain points from the eye. The trout in the stream at Mitcham Grove are numerous and large; to such as possess leave of angling from its proprietor, it must be a high treat.

"The pleasure grounds lead entirely round the meadow on the opposite side of the river, and diversify the scene, until they reach down to the extreme point on the left of the river, where they are joined by those belonging to Mr. Rutter. Though the grounds of Mitcham Grove terminate here, the river, gliding in a direct course, appears as if emerging from the confines of a wood, and seen through the various openings and vistas, leads to a belief of the other premises belonging to the same property; nor is the deception detected, until you reach the point of the lawn at the back of the mansion.[66]

Mitcham Grove and the Lubbocks

The buyer of the Mitcham Grove estate in 1828 was Sir John Lubbock, head of the banking firm of John Lubbock and Company. Born in 1773 into an old Norfolk family, he lived for a time at High Elms, near Farnborough, Kent, but finding it inconvenient for travelling to the City had been attracted to Mitcham Grove, only 9½ miles from the Royal Exchange on a good turnpike road. Sir John is said to have driven from Mitcham to his bank in a four-in-hand, and to have been in the habit of sitting in the parlour in his top-boots, a foible which apparently caused some comment in the area. Sir John was not to become as involved in local affairs as Henry Hoare – indeed, it would have been difficult for anyone to have equalled the latter in this respect – but he took his part, serving on some committees, including that of the National Schools, and in 1831 an account was opened at his bank for the deposit of the poor rate money.

Sir John's only son, also named John, was born in 1803, and by 1825 he had become a partner in the bank. An outstanding mathematician, he later became the first chancellor of London University, one of the treasurers of the Great Exhibition of 1851, and a member of numerous scientific commissions. His eldest child, another John, was born in 1834, and was destined to become even more famous than his father. A great deal of his early childhood was spent at Mitcham Grove with his grandparents, and the impact of these idyllic surroundings in the formative years of his life must have been an important factor in his subsequent development as a renowned naturalist. The Wandle, at that time still a clear stream abounding in fine trout despite increasing pollution from tanneries and other industries at Beddington, ran through the extensive and beautiful grounds of the house. Beyond the gates lay the village of Mitcham, situated in the centre of hundreds of acres of arable farmland, herb gardens, woodland and open heath. The scene moved Hassell to remark how in late summer the hues of the herbage were "particularly diversified". There was "blue from the ripe lavender, red and brown from the herbs, rich dark yellow from the wheat, pale yellow and greens of various casts from ripe and unripe barley and oats, purples from the seed clovers, and deep brown from the fallow lands". Given such an environment, and the devoted encouragement of both father and grandfather, the little boy encountered few obstacles to the development of his great interest in all aspects of the life which abounded around him.

What was doubtless a source of wonder and curiosity was the arrival at Mitcham Grove in 1838 of the first devices ever to reach England for the taking of Daguerreotype photographs which the inventor, Daguerre, had forwarded from France to Sir John Lubbock. In later years his grandson claimed he had assisted in (or had perhaps hindered!) the taking of the first picture ever to be recorded by the sun in England.

On the death of Sir John in 1840 the family returned to High Elms, and Mitcham Grove ceased to be the family home; this is confirmed by the 1841 census return, which shows only three persons resident in the mansion, a manservant and two maids. Five years later, advertisements having failed to secure a purchaser at a satisfactory price, Mitcham Grove had been demolished and the materials sold.[67] When the tithe commutation survey was conducted in 1846, only the site of the house was recorded, surrounded by 22 acres of gardens and shrubberies. The sole buildings left standing from Henry Hoare's time were the hothouse, the stables and outbuildings, and a gatekeeper's lodge. The passing of this fine house, so long associated with the local community and the home of some of its most distinguished residents, must have left a serious gap in village life. Adjustment to the loss would have been made all the more difficult by the chronically depressed state of Mitcham's two staple industries of textile printing and physic gardening.

In 1846 the grounds of Mitcham Grove were still owned by Sir John Lubbock, the third baronet, but very shortly afterwards they were amongst the 160 acres of land on either side of the river purchased by George Parker Bidder, then living at the nearby Mitcham Hall. Until the end of the century the Grove formed part of the grounds of 'Ravensbury Park', the new house Bidder erected for himself off the Sutton Road. Break-up of the estate followed the death of his eldest son in 1896, but a plot on the south bank of the river, overlooking the site of Mitcham Grove, was retained and used for the erection of Harold F Bidder's 'Ravensbury Manor' in 1912.

The northern fringe of the Grove estate bordering Morden Road contained good deposits of sand and gravel, and these were exploited by the Bidders. In doing so they were instrumental in uncovering the southern part of the famous Anglo-Saxon cemetery of Mitcham. This important Dark Age site, dating to the period AD 450-600, contained the graves of several hundred men and women, many of them buried with their weapons and jewellery. A considerable number of the graves was excavated between 1891 and 1922, mainly under the supervision of Harold Bidder, who was an active amateur archaeologist. What was found cast an important new light on the post-Roman period in this part of the Wandle valley, the significance of which is still not fully understood.[68]

As the grandson of Sir John Lubbock spent much of his early childhood at his grandfather's house, Mitcham can claim some interest in his later career – in fact, he never entirely deserted the village, for there are entries in his diaries recording the many games of golf played there until 1906, when he was 72. Leaving Eton at the early age of 14, he at once entered the family bank. The position was no sinecure, however, for shortly after his arrival the partners died and he, with his father and one old clerk, carried on the business. Banking did not by any means absorb all his energies or interests, and as the years passed he became famous in many spheres, including those of natural history, geology and literature. In 1870 he entered Parliament, and at once pressed for reforms in shop hours and elementary education, and proposed his Bank Holiday Bill for a general day's holiday to be given to all workers. It is when one reads that one of his aims was that no young person under the age of 18 should work more than 72 hours per week that one realises how much has been achieved in the last century to shorten working hours.

John Lubbock's campaign for shop assistants progressed very slowly against a great deal of opposition, and it was not until 30 years later that his Early Closing Bill – for the majority of shops to close at 8 o'clock in the evening – became law. It is surprising, therefore, that his Bank Holiday Bill met with few obstructions and was passed in 1871 to the great delight of workers of all kinds. The press of the day carried full reports of the excitement and the excursions which took place on the occasion of the first Bank Holiday, adding that on all sides blessings were called on Sir John's name. (His father having died in 1865, he had succeeded to the baronetcy.) There were even half-serious suggestions that the day should be called "St Lubbock's day"! Special trains were run and Londoners in their tens of thousands poured to the coast or onto the river boats for a day in the open air. Opposition to the holiday developed, however, and continued for many years on the grounds that it increased drunkenness. Eventually a count was made of 'drunks' at three of the London termini, but although the number was small the accusation continued to be made, fortunately with no effect. Among other bills introduced by Sir John Lubbock were those for a weekly half-holiday for shop-assistants, for the establishment of public libraries, and for the formation of open spaces in large cities. At one time he was lecturing and writing both as a naturalist and geologist. A great reader himself, he published a list of "One Hundred Good Books". "Never be without a book", he advised his son when they were once travelling together, and thereupon produced a book from his own pocket and became immersed in it for the rest of the journey.

Sir John was created Lord Avebury in 1900 and died in 1913 at the age of 79. With his death there passed what was probably the last link with the great days of Mitcham Grove.

Finis

Although an old coach house and the lodge remained tenanted for many years after the demolition of Mitcham Grove, the extensive grounds were never again occupied solely as an adjunct of a gentleman's house. For over 50 years nothing of interest was recorded locally touching upon the history of the estate, but by the end of the 19th century several changes occurred. At about the time Harold Bidder was busy with the excavation of the Dark Age cemetery, the southern part of the grounds was in the occupation of a Mr Jenner, who lived at 'Wandle House', another former Hoare property on the eastern side of the London Road. Jenner was a trotting enthusiast, and is said to have indulged his love of the sport by laying out a trotting track encircling the lawns which once surrounded Mitcham Grove.[54]

Changes were also occurring in the northern half of the grounds, in addition to gravel digging, and in 1901 the old walled gardens and a few outbuildings remaining from Sir John Lubbock's time were taken over by the silent film company of Cricks and Sharp. An empty cottage was used as offices and a laboratory, and one of the old greenhouses, suitably blacked out, for developing and printing. Comic shorts were a speciality, and many of the sequences were filmed 'on location' on (or in) the Wandle. Mitcham residents were enlisted as extras for the crowd scenes, enticed by the promise of a couple of pints of beer and half-a-crown for the day. Stars, it is said, were not much called for, and Jenner's daughter would sometimes play the heroine.

The film studios were acquired by Hovis and Company during the first World War, and their site was gradually lost beneath a complex of office buildings and workshops used by Locomotors, an associated company specialising in the manufacture of commercial vehicle bodies and later the servicing of electrically-powered delivery vehicles. The remaining portion of Mitcham Grove, including the unspoilt parkland adjoining the Wandle, was purchased by Hovis for a company sports ground in 1923. The lawns became the cricket field, in the centre of which, in times of drought, parched grass outlined the foundations of Henry Hoare's villa, still surviving a few inches below the surface.

In June 1973 it was announced in the local press that after 60 years in Mitcham Locomotors were closing the works down and relocating production in Andover. The move followed the take-over of the firm, a subsidiary of the Rank, Hovis, McDougall Group, by British United Engineering the previous year, and was justified on 'economic grounds'. Resettlement assistance was offered to the workforce, but many declined to move away from Mitcham and there was a predictable outcry from the unions. The decision had been taken, however, and the works closed, those not relocating receiving redundancy payments.

Twelve months later, having granted outline planning consent for use of the land for housing, the London Borough of Merton purchased the derelict works and the adjoining sports field for £1m. The proposal to use the land for the erection of a new 160-unit showpiece municipal housing estate was the 'brainchild' of Councillor David Chalkley, then chairman of the Housing Committee. The action was criticised by the Conservative opposition as over-hasty and grossly extravagant, but the majority party was not to be deflected, holding "the needs of the homeless" to be paramount and that the Council had a duty to put the

The Cricket Pitch, 'Hovis' Sportsground, London Road, Mitcham
(ENM 1969)

land to public use rather than "let it get into the hands of unscrupulous property speculators". Plans were soon produced for a high density low rise estate based on the design first seen at Pollards Hill, where it won an RIBA award for the Borough Architect's team headed by Bernard Ward, and later at Eastfields.

Difficulties were soon encountered through the number of watercourses traversing the site, and its liability to flooding. A backwater of the Wandle and a culvert across the site had to be accommodated and, to reduce the danger of the new estate being flooded, four acres were required to be set aside for a lake to hold water should the river level rise after prolonged rainfall. Consequently, fewer dwellings than originally planned were built. As the new Watermeads estate neared completion it was stated in the press that costs per unit would be £18,881 each, and that, with a subsidy of £37.60 per week, rents were calculated to range from £5.46 to £8.24. The lake, attractively landscaped and incorporated in a linear park linking the National Trust's Watermeads and Ravensbury Park, today provides an extremely attractive setting for the estate.

The Watermeads estate (ENM 1990)
The cedar tree once stood on the lawn of Mitcham Grove

GROVE HOUSE

Crescent Grove and the shop and houses numbered 494 to 512 London Road Mitcham stand on a site which, until the late 1920s, had been occupied by at least two substantial houses, the last of which is now beyond the memory of all but the oldest local residents.

The first house of which we have evidence was of 18th-century date, or possibly earlier, and was surrounded by several acres of garden, orchard and paddocks.[1] During the 1780s and '90s it was the home of Penelope Woodcock,[2] whose husband's family had been resident in Mitcham for upwards of a century, George Woodcock, her father-in-law, being appointed as one of the trustees "for the poore bread" by the vestry in 1703.[3] George Woodcock was a whitster by trade, bleaching calicoes and linens for the printing works which abounded along the Wandle valley at that time. The business seems to have been profitable, and the Woodcocks enjoyed a respectable niche in the village during their lifetime. Both George Woodcock and his son Thomas held various parish offices, and in 1792 Penelope, by this time widowed, presented the newly erected Sunday School building on Lower Green West with a turret clock, which can still be seen above the central pediment over the front entrance door.[4]

We have no idea of the appearance of the Woodcocks' house, but it was described as "genteel" by Edwards, using an epithet he reserved for houses of varying size to convey to his readers that the furnishings were tasteful and the property well-maintained.[5] For land tax purposes the house and land was assessed at £55 p.a, based on the estimated rental value in 1780, which suggests a residence of more than average size for the village. The ground landlord was Lord Loughborough of Mitcham Grove who, as we have seen, was to sell the estate, including the Woodcocks' house, to Henry Hoare in 1786.

As Lot 2 the freehold house and 13 acres of land were sold for £2,960 when the estate of the late Henry Hoare was auctioned in 1828. It was then occupied by a "Mr. Smith", who held it on an 11-year lease from Michaelmas 1817. The sale particulars describe the house as a "desirable residence with forecourt, enclosed from the road by a wall and pallisade". On the ground floor, off "a neat entrance hall" were breakfast parlour, drawing room and dining parlour, each papered and with marble fireplaces. A kitchen and scullery (the latter with a pump of water) completed the ground floor. There were four "excellent bed chambers" on the first floor, and a servants' bedroom reached by a secondary staircase. Outside, the domestic offices comprised a washhouse-cum-brewhouse with oven, a chaise house, 'coal hole', a cart house, a four-stall stable, cowhouse, hen house and piggery. Flower and kitchen gardens, orchard and meadowland completed what must have been virtually a self-contained establishment.[6] Whether or not it was the house the Woodcocks knew, we cannot say.

"Mr. Smith" was George Smith, the architect responsible for the design of Mitcham parish church, rebuilt between 1819 and 1822. He was born at Aldenham, Herts, in 1782, and after being articled to R. F. Brettingham in 1797 had become a clerk to James Wyatt in 1802. Smith exhibited at the Royal Academy from 1801 until 1849, was a Fellow of the Society of Antiquaries and also of the Institute of British Architects, of which he was Vice-President in 1844-5. In 1810 Smith was appointed district surveyor to the southern division of the City of London, and in

Grove House c.1910

1814 surveyor to the Mercers' Company, retaining both posts until his death in 1869. Some of his principal works were Whittington's Almshouses in Highgate, St Paul's School, and the Corn Exchange in Mark Lane.[7] In 1815 George Smith came to reside at Mitcham, leasing Tamworth Lodge, off Commonside East, from Daniel Watney. In 1818 he had been appointed by Mitcham vestry to conduct a survey and valuation for rating purposes of property in the parish, and it was his report on the structural condition of the old medieval church that influenced the decision to demolish and rebuild in 1819.

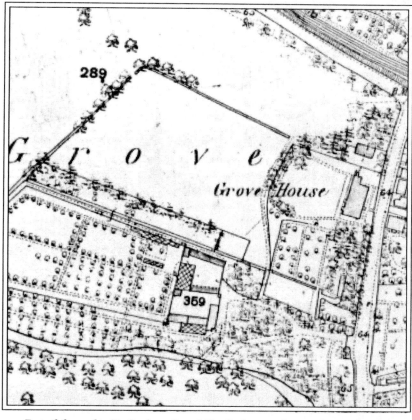

Detail from the Six Inch to One Mile Ordnance Survey Map of 1867,
showing 'Grove House'

Although he had vacated the property some time previously, it was still known as "Mr. Smith's house" when bought by George Parker Bidder in 1846. It was then in the occupation of a Louisa Dean, a widow,[8] and was almost certainly held on a lease from the trustees of Sir John Lubbock, the previous owner of the Mitcham Grove estate. Louisa Dean was the sister of Thomas Rutter, the retired tobacco and snuff manufacturer whose family operated the Ravensbury snuff mills. By 1851 Louisa Dean's son, Lloyd, who was living with her, had followed his uncle into the business.[9] Whether he was at the Ravensbury mills with Isaac Campbell Rutter and John Rutter III, or worked at the company's London premises, is not known. The Rutter family remained prominent in Mitcham and Morden well into the early years of the next century, but the Deans seem to have vacated Grove House sometime in the 1850s.

The next occupiers of whom we have trace are John Harrison Stanton and his wife Elizabeth, eldest surviving daughter of George Parker Bidder.[10] The couple were married at Morden in 1859, and what appears as 'Grove House' on the Ordnance map of 1865-7 is said to have been erected to John Stanton's design. The son of a Newcastle solicitor, he had been indentured to Robert Stephenson, and later worked for him as an assistant on the Egyptian railway, where he met 'Lizzie' Bidder, who was visiting Egypt in the winter of 1858/9. They raised a large family – 13 children in all – at Grove House, and eventually moved away to Stubb House, County Durham, which Stanton inherited from an uncle.[11]

By the time the Ordnance Survey revision of 1894 was conducted, Grove House had become known as 'Mitcham Grove House', and it was described as the seat of Mrs George Gibb shortly before the outbreak of war in 1914.[12] Prominent members of the parish church, George and Constance Gibb were responsible for the gift of the *voix céleste* and new tremulant stops which were added to the organ in 1910. Mitcham Grove House seems to have survived as a private house until the 1920s, ending its days as the private 'Ravensbury School'. It was demolished in the early 1930s to prepare the site for the erection of the present houses, the school transferring to a large weatherboarded house on the opposite side of the London Road, at one time associated with the long-defunct Mitcham Brewery.

RAVENSBURY AND THE ORIGINS OF MITCHAM

No study of the history of the Ravensbury area would be complete without something being said of the large post-Roman or 'Anglo-Saxon' cemetery excavated by Harold Bidder and members of his family between 1888 and 1922. A definitive article by John Morris on the cemetery and the grave goods recovered has appeared in the *Surrey Archaeological Collections*,[1] and it is therefore not the intention of the writer to attempt to cover this ground again, although with 60 years having elapsed, some of Morris's conclusions now seem questionable.

It is important, however, to consider what the evidence can lead us to deduce about the early history of the village of Mitcham.

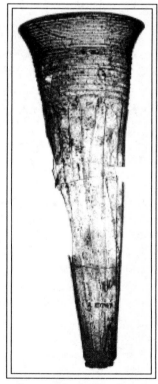

The main concentration of burials lay either side of the Morden Road, between Mitcham station and Ravensbury Park, but other interments have been found to the north, almost as far as the parish church. This suggests the burial site observed Roman custom, and lay outside the principal settlement, which may have been where a circular ditched enclosure has been identified to the south of the medieval church. It had been known for well over a century before the Bidders' excavations that human remains were to be found at Ravensbury, and one of the fields was known as 'Dead Man's Close'. Workmen digging liquorice roots for herb growers Potter and Moore on land to the north of the road in 1848 unearthed a large number of bones, together with swords, spear heads, glass beakers and brooches, and the interest that these discoveries aroused amongst Victorian antiquaries was

Green glass beaker from Mitcham, reproduced by courtesy of Museum of London

recounted by Ben Slater in his memoirs many years later.[2] The full significance of the finds was not appreciated at that time, and it was not until Harold Bidder took advantage of his family's ownership of the former Mitcham Grove and Ravensbury estates, and the opportunity afforded by the excavation of the sand and gravel deposits lying beneath the fields and meadows bordering the Morden Road, that the extent and significance of the cemetery came to be realised.

Through the work of archaeologists over the last century, and the reporting of various stray finds, it has become evident that during the 350 years of the Roman period the Wandle valley remained widely settled by predominantly native British communities. Stane Street, the road from London to Chichester constructed around AD70, passed through Colliers Wood in what later became the northern part of the parish of Mitcham, crossed the Wandle at Merton and, after rising over the hill at Morden, continued on its course to Ewell and beyond. From the vicinity of the road, and to the south at Carshalton, Beddington and Croydon, we have numerous finds of pottery, coins, and burials, which are indicative of a substantial, if scattered, population. At Beddington there was also a villa, complete with bath-house, stock yard and barn, erected in about 180 AD in place of an earlier timber farmhouse. This, in its turn, had replaced a group of typical round houses of the late Iron Age.[3]

Barely a mile to the north of Ravensbury, on what was to become the Lombard Road factory estate, the discovery in 1922 of coins, pottery and building material suggested the existence of a settlement at the side of the Roman road.[4] Evidence of other homesteads or farms has come from sites off Willow Lane, Church Road and Western Road at Mitcham,[5] whilst a partially excavated Romano-British cemetery exists between Church Road and Phipps Bridge.[6] Within recent years, further discoveries have been made in the Ravensbury area itself, the excavations by Surrey Archaeological Society prior to the erection of the Watermeads housing estate in 1974/5[7] producing a handful of sherds of Romano-British origin and a piece of decorated bone, and in 1989 more pottery of the 2nd/3rd century came from a ditch feature exposed by a team from the Museum of London working on a site to the south of Mitcham parish church.[8]

Unfortunately archaeology so far has tantalisingly little to tell of life in the neighbourhood of Ravensbury or, indeed, elsewhere in north-eastern Surrey in the closing years of the Roman period. We have scarcely any evidence from the known settlement sites that occupation continued beyond the mid-4th century and, apart from Ravensbury, no burials that have been recognised as late Roman or Saxon. The coins found on the line of Stane Street at Merton indicate that money may still have been in use as a medium of exchange at the settlement here possibly until the end of the 4th century, for the latest coin found, of Valentinian I and dated to AD 375, could have been in circulation some years after it had been minted. (Very little Roman coinage found its way to Britain after the turn of the century, and the monetary system had probably broken down completely by *c.*420.) If road-side trading continued at Merton into the early 5th century, and there is no reason to believe that it did not, transactions would of necessity have been based increasingly on a system of exchange in which coins played no part, and which left no archaeological evidence.

Many attempts have been made at a satisfactory explanation for the paucity of evidence from the late 4th century, and the virtual disappearance of the Romano-British from the archaeological record in the early 5th century. The absence of coinage and commercially produced pottery has undoubtedly made dating more difficult, and a reversion to timber and thatch rather than brick and tile for domestic buildings would render settlements less easy to recognise. Some writers have suggested an actual decline in the population brought about by lower living standards and disease, but this is not easily substantiated. Whereas there may be some justification for broadly accepting what Gildas, the 6th-century historian, recounted of the devastation and horrors which accompanied the Saxon migration into southern Britain in the latter part of the 5th century, in recent years various writers have questioned whether the destruction and slaughter were as widespread or cataclysmic as Gildas would have had his readers believe. The theory has also been advanced for periods of relative stability and co-existence between the British and the earliest Saxon settlers before the struggle for supremacy commenced around 450. At least initially, the newcomers could only have represented a minority amongst a substantially British population. The main preoccupation of both groups would have been subsistence farming, and with pressure no longer exerted to grow a surplus of corn and other produce to meet Imperial taxes, there could well have been a surfeit of potentially arable land.

There would thus seem to have been little reason for serious conflict between the indigenous population of the south-east and the immigrant Saxon families, and one can imagine a degree of cultural fusion and intermarriage eventually taking place. Evidence which seems to support this belief has come from several sites. There are, for instance, the claims for sherds of late Romano-British pottery being found in close association with early Saxon material at Carshalton and Waddon, whilst complete pots of Romano-British manufacture were found in graves in the Saxon cemetery at Croydon. What is of particular significance for us, a few coins and several other objects of indisputable Roman origin were interred with the dead in the 'Anglo-Saxon' cemetery at Ravensbury.

There is, therefore, a case not only for arguing continuity of occupation of the Wandle valley beyond the collapse of Roman Britain, but also for the survival of a substantial element of native British amongst the population well into the 5th century and beyond. It also seems reasonable to assume that these people, British and Saxon alike, were to be found living in hamlets and farmsteads scattered across the more fertile soils of the river terraces. Moreover one suspects, but cannot yet prove, that the villages with Early English place-names like 'Totinge', 'Stretham', 'Mordon' and 'Bedinton', which begin to emerge in the documentary record by the late 7th century, were continuing the broad pattern of settlement already well established in the Roman period.

The earliest archaeological evidence for a Saxon presence in Mitcham comes from the Ravensbury cemetery. One of the largest in Surrey, this appears on the evidence of the grave goods to have been in use for a period of some 150 years, at least two interments in Morris's estimation being from early in the 5th century, whilst the latest took place a little before 600. Over half the 238 burials recorded were dated by the reported associated finds, composed mainly of weapons, belt fastenings, brooches and other articles in distinctive Saxon styles. Some burials unaccompanied by grave goods could well lie outside this range, and of

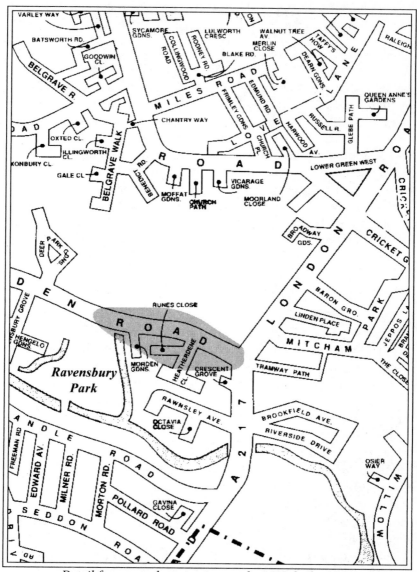

*Detail from a modern street map, showing the location
of the 'Dark Age' cemetery at Ravensbury, reproduced by
permission of Merton Design Unit, London Borough of Merton
The shaded area indicates the main area of burials*

course nothing can be said of the many hundreds robbed or destroyed without record in the past.

The very important question of the actual identity of the people buried here has not so far received much attention. The assumption made by Bidder and Morris, on the evidence of the weapons and most of the grave goods, was that they were 'Anglo-Saxons', but this is not necessarily true in all cases. The fact that many of the men carried weapons of the type common amongst the Saxons, and the women favoured jewellery fashioned in the style of or popularised by Saxon craftsmen did not determine their ethnicity beyond doubt. No such assumption could be made with regard to those buried without possessions and, except in a few rare cases where the excavators noted a stratigraphical relationship with a datable grave, they could not be dated. Morris concluded these burials were merely of poor people, and may well have been correct, but it might also be argued that they represent a separate element in the community, members of which observed a different funerary tradition.

It is noticeable that the majority of the inhumations were orientated with feet to the East, following Christian and late Roman custom. Morris commented that this is also the predominant orientation in pagan Saxon cemeteries, the practice, he said, being copied from the Romans. The majority of the Mitcham 'Saxons' would thus appear to be conforming to an established, and presumably local, custom. It is also interesting that whereas cremation was the practice in the Saxon homelands, no evidence whatever of cremation burials was reported from the Mitcham cemetery. Finally, there is the very important question raised by the handful of graves producing Roman material, which included fragments of pottery, a belt fitting and bronze finger-rings, coins and a beautiful 4th century glass amphora. Many of the graves discovered by farm workers in the mid-19th century are also said to have contained coins (presumably Roman), which were sold to dealers. It is unfortunate that so much of the cemetery was destroyed before its significance was recognised, and that none of it was dug with the benefit of modern archaeological techniques. A few burials may still remain undisturbed, and one can only hope that if and when they are discovered, it will be possible for them to be examined properly. The implications of what we do know about the cemetery are obvious, however – some of the burials at Mitcham could have been of late Roman date, and use of the cemetery continued into the 5th century by people of both Romano-British and Saxon origins.

Morris formed the opinion that, if the Mitcham cemetery remained in use for any appreciable time after 600, it must have served an impoverished community, who interred their dead without possessions. An alternative explanation could be that some of the burials which so inconveniently lacked datable grave goods, were in fact post-600, and that they were reflecting further changes taking place in funerary practice under the renewed influence of Christianity, which had returned to Surrey by the mid-7th century. Mellitus had become Bishop of London in 604, and Chertsey Abbey, which was founded in 666, claimed to have held an estate in Mitcham as early as 675.[9] Given the missionary zeal of the early Roman Church, charged by Pope Gregory with the task of bringing the Gospel to the heathen English (many hundreds of whom were claimed to have been baptised by St Augustine in 597) it is to be expected that priests from the minster church of St Peter at Chertsey would soon have been active amongst its tenants in Mitcham.

The number and concentration of burials in the cemetery led Morris to conclude it served a compact village rather than a number of scattered farms each with its small family graveyard. This need not have been the case, and other authorities have suggested that large cemeteries might have served communities scattered over the surrounding areas. However, accepting Morris's hypothesis, we may imagine the village to which the Mitcham cemetery belonged as a somewhat random grouping of houses of various sizes and types, resembling the 'Dark Age' settlements now known from a number of excavations in the south-east of England.[10] On the assumption that some 400-500 burials had taken place over a period of 150 years, Morris furthermore suggested the village at Mitcham could hardly have been a large one, and visualised a community of from 50 to 100 persons, perhaps increasing in size towards the end of the 6th century, and living in a cluster of a score or so houses. With so much still unknown this is, of course, little more than guesswork.

In 1989 the excavations conducted by the Museum of London Archaeological Service to the south of Mitcham church exposed features which may have been part of a roughly circular ditched enclosure. Apart from the Romano-British material already mentioned, some late Saxon pottery was also found. Nothing more was discovered to show that here was an actual habitation site, and what slight archaeological evidence of structures which might have survived, given the nature of the buildings at the time, is now likely to have been severely disturbed, if not destroyed. The site is, however, the focal point of a number of old lanes and field paths, which points to it having been of some significance in the past, and further excavation might yet be productive.

Who, then, were the people whose descendants have given us the names for Mitcham and the neighbouring villages, and what were the circumstances that induced them to settle in this part of Surrey? The historical record is of little use in reconstructing a reliable backcloth to the 5th century, but it is known that for well over a century south-eastern Britain had attracted land-hungry migrants sailing from the Low Countries and the north German coast. The Kent and Sussex coasts had long been subjected to forays by sea-borne raiders entering the river estuaries, and landing on the gently sloping beaches. Whilst the shore forts were manned, and the province was still garrisoned by Imperial forces, immigration could be controlled, but the situation must have changed rapidly once the regular troops were withdrawn. The Thames, of course, gave ready access to north-eastern Surrey, whence Roman roads led inland, and the archaeological evidence is for quite small numbers of migrants, either as individuals or family groups, finding their way to the Wandle valley by the early 5th century. Here they might have discovered land which had been abandoned – an example of the *agri deserti* common elsewhere in the Empire, and complained of by Roman writers. The buildings of Beddington villa appear to have fallen into decay by the latter part of the 4th century, and part of the estate may have been left to revert to scrub. The same process could quite possibly have been occurring in parts of Mitcham, but the fertile soils bordering the Wandle are more likely to have remained in cultivation.

The Ravensbury cemetery, together with that at Croydon, has a number of grave-goods contemporary with some of the earliest Saxon migrants.

Bede's *Adventus Saxonium* ought certainly no longer to be regarded as a unique and closely datable event which took place in or about 450, but rather as the culmination of a prolonged period of folk migration. Morris supported the view that the Mitcham Saxons, and their kin at Beddington and Croydon, had been settled here when the British invited German federates, as a deliberate act of policy, to help defend the southern approaches to London in the mid-5th century. If this did take place, the evidence suggests it would have been as a reinforcement of established communities. Morris saw these three cemeteries of the Wandle valley as situated on the nearest inhabited land to the south-west of London, but excavations at Clapham have since shown this assumption to be untrue.[11] One suspects that Saxon settlement to the south of London in the early 5th century will eventually be found to have been far more widespread than was once believed. Morris went on to stress what he saw as the strategic significance of the three settlements: "Placed on the Wandle between Merton and Croydon, these garrisons blocked all access to London from the south. They covered the London-Chichester and London-Brighton roads at the two Roman roadside villages nearest to London."[12] The idea has an initial romantic attraction, but presupposes the continued existence into the mid-5th century of a British authority in the London region capable not only of strategic planning, but exercising control over an area extending some 10-12 miles into Surrey. So little is known of London at this time that it is impossible to say if such a body existed. Some activity continued to the west of the city, however, for traders in the London area retained commercial contact with the mainland of Europe into the mid-5th century, and Gaulish merchants were trading with London as late as 468.

The 'evidence' of place-names in support of the theory of continuity of occupation is, of course, to be treated with great caution,[13] but locally we have some fascinating examples. The derivation of 'Wallington' from the Old English Waletona or Waleton(e) – 'weal tun' or farm of the 'Welsh', i.e. Celtic British[14] – is certainly interesting and does lend support to the belief that an identifiable enclave of people of Romano-British stock was still to be found in the vicinity of Mitcham until well into the 7th or 8th centuries.[15] The hundred of Wallington, which embraced Mitcham and the spring line settlements from Cheam to

Croydon, and remained a focus for local fiscal and judicial purposes until the 20th century, is a typical example of a place-name providing evidence of a primitive grouping of estates or land units about a central point, the meeting place of the hundred moot, and hints at an administrative framework perhaps dating to the sub-Roman period.

From Mitcham itself we seem to have a further hint of continuity, although not so immediately apparent. As we have seen in chapter I, the vill of 'Witford' was recorded in the Domesday survey of 1086, and recurs as 'Wicford' (in various spellings preserving the hard 'c or 'k' sound) in documents throughout the 12th and 13th centuries.[16] In 1362, as 'Wykeford',[17] it was synonymous with Lower Mitcham, bordering the Wandle.

The evident persistence of the 'wic(k)' form of the name throughout the middle ages ('Witford' or 'Whitford' did not reappear until the 18th century) suggests that phonetically this was closest to the more usual spoken form, and that the local English rendering had been modified by the Norman clerks when compiling the Domesday record. One is therefore justified in proceeding further on the premise that the 'wic' element is, in fact, Old English, and predates the Conquest.

Aware of the alternative form of the name, Gover and others[14] suggested Whitford might be interpreted as 'ford by the wic'. Whereas 'wic' can denote a dairy farm, it also has a clear association with the Latin *vicus* – a term for a very variable unit in Roman times, ranging from a small town to a settlement, and which by the end of the 4th century may have come to include a village. Research has shown that a large proportion of the 'wick' names in England, often occurring in combination with other elements, are either on or close to a Roman road, or less than half a mile from sites known to have been occupied during the Roman period. Many are found to actually coincide with Romano-British settlement sites.[18] It is a reasonable hypothesis, therefore, given the archaeological evidence from Mitcham, that the term 'wic-ford' was applied to a Wandle crossing in the proximity of the former Romano-British *vicus*, and that in subsequent common usage its meaning was extended to include the general area on the north bank of the river in the vicinity of the river, as well as the ford itself.

The first Anglo-Saxon settlers seem to have begun to arrive in the district early in the 5th century, and by the mid-7th century the area of settlement was sufficiently extensive to merit the name of 'Micham' in contemporary deeds. In this, its earliest form, the name Mitcham contains firstly the Old English element 'micel', meaning 'big'. The second element could be either 'ham' or 'hamm'; the two are difficult to distinguish, and have different meanings. 'Ham' can be interpreted as 'village', 'place', or even 'home', and may also be used in the sense of an estate. 'Hamm', on the other hand, was used variously as meaning land in a riverbend, or on a promontory, or dry ground in a marsh, a river meadow or a cultivated plot in marginal land, or a piece of valley bottom land hemmed in by higher ground. 'Micham' can thus be seen as conveying the idea of a large expanse of arable land and water meadows enclosed by a bend in the river. The absence of an early spelling of Mitcham ending with a double 'm' need not concern us here, for study of the topography is the important factor in recognition of the origin of this form. Even today, the description still seems particularly apt as, when approaching Mitcham from the south, one descends the incline from Rose Hill to cross the Wandle beside the old ford. What remains of the village centre, near the parish church and clustered round the Lower Green, can be seen to lie at the heart of a broad expanse of level ground some two miles wide, beyond which rise the hills of Streatham and Norwood.

If our interpretation is correct, this places Mitcham in what Gelling calls the 'topographical' settlement-name classification – the type describing the physical setting rather than the 'habitative', which uses a word for a settlement. The translation of 'Mitcham' as 'big home' or 'big place', generally favoured by local historians in the past, does now seem to be less feasible than a topographical derivation. Moreover, contrary to the assumptions of authorities at the beginning of the 20th century, the topographical form of place-name is now seen as the earliest type, illustrative of the importance physical factors played in the selection of habitation sites.[19] This accords well with our present understanding of the origins of Mitcham.

Tradition does tell us of stiffening British resistance to further Saxon insurrections and incursions into central southern Britain during the mid-

5th century, commencing with the campaigns initiated by Ambrosius Aurelianus, the *dux bellorum* of noble birth described by Gildas, and culminating in Arthur's victory at Mount Badon in about 500. Welsh and English tradition also holds that the country was to enjoy relative peace and freedom from foreign invasion for a further 50 years, although squabbling continued intermittently amongst the British themselves.

Arthur is said to have died at Camlann in about 515, and the stability won at Badon had evidently collapsed by the middle of the 6th century. The British appear to have lacked any central cohesion, and Gildas, writing about 540, says they had five kings or princelings. The old Roman province of Britannia had by now disintegrated and Procopius, who wrote some ten years later, describes the British as subject to 'tyrants' or usurpers. The advance into the Midlands and the south-west continued between 550 and 600 and, succeeding in defeating the British, Saxon warlords eventually gained control of the greater part of lowland Britain. Often this may not have been so much a war between two clearly defined racial groups as a prolonged struggle between rulers of different provinces striving for supremacy.

In the south-east the kings of Wessex and Kent fought for possession of what later became north-eastern Surrey. At the battle of Wibbandune[20] between Caewlin and Cutha of Wessex and Ethelbert of Kent in 568 Caewlin was victorious, and for a time the Wandle valley may have been left in a no-man's land between the two kingdoms. This, the first sign of Kentish expansion for a hundred years, marks the beginning of a long campaign spanning much of Ethelbert's reign (560-616). Caewlin died in 593 and his nephew, Coelwulf, who succeeded to the throne of Wessex in 597, found himself in a state of continuous war with the Picts and the British, as well as the neighbouring Anglo-Saxon kingdoms.

We of course cannot tell what part, if any, the people of the middle Wandle valley played in the struggle for control of the southern Home Counties which took place between the kings of Wessex and Kent in the 6th century. From a study of the typology of the brooches found at Ravensbury, however, it seemed to Morris that during this period the inhabitants of Mitcham were able to achieve a degree of prosperity and creative independence they had not known before. During the early 6th century their jewellery was of a distinctive type, presumably made in the locality, and may have been traded far into south-western Surrey. Towards the middle of the century the situation seems to have changed, and the local brooches disappear, to be replaced by imitations, notably of Kentish design. The relative poorness of the later Mitcham jewellery, and the lack of variety to be seen in the material derived from Kent and north of the Thames, led Morris to suggest that whatever independence and prosperity the Wandle communities had enjoyed did not persist. He considered that after the middle of the 6th century "they were too poor to maintain a brooch-maker of their own, or to produce wealthy women or powerful chieftains".[21]

So far, excavation of the Ravensbury cemetery has provided nothing to carry the history of Mitcham much beyond 600. We know that by then London was in the hands of Ethelbert, and his son was king of Essex, but by the end of the 7th century the balance of power had shifted, and London lay within the kingdom of Wessex, for between 674 and 688 we find Ine, king of Wessex, referring to Erkenwald, bishop of London, as "my bishop" in the preamble to his laws.[22] Whilst the kings' struggles for supremacy swept back and forth, the main concern of the peasant farmers in the Wandle valley, was undoubtedly survival of themselves and their families, and the defence of their livestock and crops.

Saxon style brooches from Mitcham, reproduced by courtesy of Museum of London

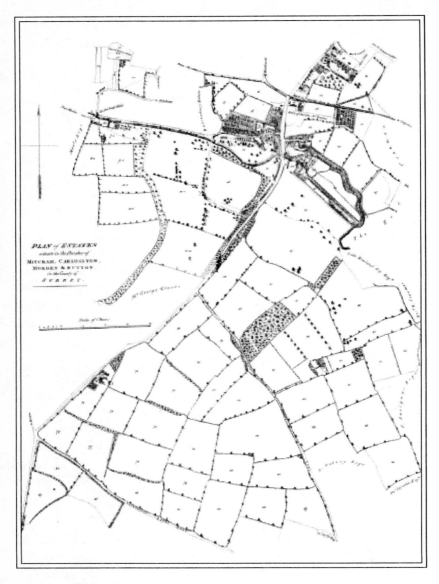

Henry Hoare's estate in 1828, from the sales particulars
reproduced by courtesy of London Borough of Sutton Archives
ref: 2361/2/2

(Appendices 1a-1c are transcripts of extracts of wills made by Doris E. Dawes)

APPENDIX 1a

Extract from Will of Susannah Smyth Spinster of Mitcham.

Will dated 13 Feb 1724, probate 30 July 1725. (Prob 11 604 162) SHC 145/46

"I give devise and bequeath all my Manors Messuages Advowsons Tythes Lands Tenements and hereditaments whatsoever to my kinsman William Myers of King Street London Gent, his heirs and assigns for ever. All my real estates in the County of Surrey to William Myers except for £1000 ..... To Damaris Myers, sister of William Myers £100 and ten pounds to buy mourning. I give to her likewise my two small Silver Salvers, my two silver candlesticks and snuffers, my two large guilt spoons and all my books ... Ten pounds unto and amongst the poor people of Mitcham ... to each and every of my servants £5 for mourning ... I give to Elizabeth Browne Widow £200 and my great silver tankard and silver plate and all my china ware or pieces of china and also the sum of one hundred pounds with which she is to provide herself with mourning ... I give to William Myers son of the above William Myers my great silver salver and silver cup ..."

APPENDIX 1b

Extract from Will of William Myers of Mitcham in the County of Surrey and of King Street in the parish of St Lawrence Jewry London Gent. Will dated thirteenth October 1739 proved at London 29th July 1742.

(Prob 11 719 226)

"I made settlement before marriage with my now wife Mary Myers ... I give over and above the settlement aforesaid the sum of one hundred pounds to buy mourning or otherwise as she shall think fit ... also one pair of silver candlesticks the set of silver casters that are in use in my house in Mitcham, the Green Calimante[1] Bed with the ffeather Bed bolster pillows blankets and Quilt therewith commonly used and wherein we usually lye when in London. I give her likewise two pair of sheets two pair of pillow beers[2] two tablecloths twelve napkins and twelve towels such as she shall choose out of what we commonly use. I likewise will and direct that she shall have all her paraphernalia Jewells and Ornaments of her Body except the Pearl necklace which was my Mothers which was not given to but lent by me to my said wife for her wearing only, it being always intended (tho of small value) to be kept as a ffamily Jewell and to go from generation to generation and for that reason I give the said necklace to my eldest son ... I give £5 to the poor of Mitcham and to St. Laurence Jewry and St. Mary Magdalen Milk St. [united parishes]. William shall have all my books and household furniture prints pictures linnen brewing vessels implements of gardening and husbandry and other utensils which shall be in or about my house at Mitcham, likewise so much of my silver plate as my executors shall think fit to reserve for him ... I desire to be very privately interred in the parish church of Mitcham as near to my pew as conveniently may be and without aschutions [sic] or other vain show or pomp. All real estate copyhold as well as freehold by virtue of Will or settlement of Sussana Smith late of Mitcham to my son William Myers ... "

APPENDIX 1c

Extract from Will of Henry Hoare of Mitcham Grove. Will dated 1st day of March 1828, proved at London 31st March 1828. (Prob. 11 1738 151)

"The last will and testament of Henry Hoare of Fleet Street in the City of London and of Mitcham Grove in the County of Surrey, Esq. which I make and publish whilst I am through the mercy of God of sound and disposing mind memory and understanding ... I desire that my remains may be buried in the vault I have lately made in Morden Churchyard and my positive injunction is that there be not any ostentatious parade at my ffuneral. I leave to the minster who shall officiate at my burial the sum of ten pounds and to the officiating clerk the sum of five pounds including and in lieu of their legal fees ... I have a power to appoint the sum of £2500 amongst my children ... now forms part of mortgage

£15000 due from Lady Caroline Damer formerly lent to the Earl of Dorchester by his then title of Lord Milton. £2500 to my only two surviving sons George Matthew Hoare and Charles James Hoare and my daughter Dame Lydia Elizabeth the wife of Sir Thomas Acland Bart. to be divided amongst them share and share alike. I give and devise all my severall ffreehold houses ground rents and other ffreehold hereditaments in and near Exchange Alley in the City of London and also the land tax payable in respect therefore which I have redeemed and also all that Manor of Little Spilsel and the farm and lands situate at Staplehurst in the County of Kent which I have lately purchased of John Ballard ... to the use of my grandson Henry Hoare son of my dear departed son William Henry Hoare his heirs and assigns for ever ... I give devise and bequeath all and singular my ffreehold and leasehold messuages ffarms lands and other tenements and other hereditaments situate lying and being in the parishes or places of Mitcham Morden Carshalton Sutton or elsewhere in the County of Surrey and also all the rest and residue of my manors messuages ffarms lands tenements and hereditaments whatsoever and wheresoever and whether in possession reversion remainder or expectancy with their respective appurtenances unto Charles Hoare of ffleet Street aforesaid and of Dawlish in the County of Devon Esq. Henry Merrick Hoare of York Place in the parish of St. Marylebone in the County of Middlesex Esq. my said sons George Matthew Hoare and Charles James Hoare and their heirs upon trust that they shall do as they or he in their or his absolute discretion shall think fit after my decease shall sell and dispose of the same either by public auction or private contracts in lots or otherwise and shall apply and dispose of the money to arise by such sale in the manner hereinafter mentioned. All investments etc. to be for Henry Hoare ... I direct that the rents and profits of my real estates shall until sale and subject to the enjoyment of my said sons or either of them of my Mansion House at Mitcham and the gardens and pleasure grounds adjacent thereto go and be employed in the same manner as the interest etc. ... My two sons George Matthew Hoare and Charles James Hoare and the survivor of them shall have the use and occupation of my Mansion House at Mitcham and the gardens etc. for the space of six calender months from my decease and of the furniture table linen plate books china liquors wines and stores for housekeeping and shall be allowed the sum of £1000 for the maintaining thereof ... £40 to the Rev. Richard Cranmer of Mitcham, £200 to my servant Edward Longworthy to all servants who have lived with me 6 years previously to my death six months wages over and above what shall be due from me to them ... to Mr William Giles of Mitcham the sum of four hundred pounds over and above what may be due to him for his salary which I direct shall be paid to the day of my death. I recommend him to my Executors to be employed in the settlement of my books as he is a person whose integrity can be relied on and I recommend his assistance to my sons in the inspection of my papers if they shall think fit. I give to the trustees of the Mitcham Sunday School the sum of one hundred pounds to the churchwardens and overseers of the poor of the parish of Carshalton the sum of £30. £12 per week for the first four weeks after my decease may be distributed to poor persons by William Giles as has been usually done by him. I give all my wearing apparel and linen unto my servant Edward Longworthy. I also give to the said Henry Hoare my grandson all the books prints maps and pamphlets which shall be in and about my library and dwellinghouse at Mitcham ... Lady Oakes is to reside in the house which she now occupies at Mitcham until Christmas 1828 free of all rent and taxes ... If any person shall institute any proceedings for a more particular or any other amount or for inspection of books they shall forfeit all benefits. I give to Lady Acland all my paintings and portraits except the portrait of my deceased son Willam Hoare which I give to my eldest grandson Henry Hoare. I give also to him my watches watch chains seals rings jewels and trinkets".

(This is a very lengthy will and disposes of considerable property. Among other things mention is made of provision for his children under terms of a marriage settlement. I have only extracted those items which have particular local interest – D E D.)

The Edward Longworthy mentioned was Henry Hoare's valet, and he stayed with the family, becoming the grandson's butler when he married and settled in Staplehurst. (D E D)

APPENDIX 2

TREES IN RAVENSBURY PARK

(Notes Compiled by J G Berry, Deputy Director of Parks, London Borough of Merton, in September 1980)

Owing to the age of the park, it has some notable aged trees. Of these the most outstanding are the several gigantic London Plane trees, now sadly, some of them declining into senility. All of them seem to be about the same age, which has been estimated at about 200 years. They have girths at breast height of about 7.5m and heights of around 30 metres. There are also very large Oaks and Black Poplars, but none so huge as the Planes.

Most of the interesting species are on the river bank. Near the bridge on the north bank are two Ginkgo on either side of the path leading into the park proper. This species was at one time thought to be found only in Chinese temple gardens (it is a sacred tree), but more recently a grove of Ginkgos was found in a remote valley. The deciduous foliage – like huge maidenhair ferns fronds – is unique. Nearer the mill on the same bank is a Weymouth Pine, a fairly uncommon tree in the London area. Walking from the bridge towards the Watermeads on the same bank one encounters another unusual conifer, the deciduous Swamp Cypress. This tree when growing in waterlogged ground throws up 'knees' from the roots to enable them to breathe. Signs of these can be seen in the surface of the tarmac path.

A little further on is a young Western Yellow Pine. This can be identified by its long needles in big 'brushes' at the ends of stout twigs. Nearby is the remnant of an ancient Indian Bean tree. These old plants were originally shoots springing from the ruins of the parent tree – now completely decayed. This species flowers in late summer, and the long seed pods are a conspicuous feature of the tree in autumn.

Near the point where a side stream leaves the main river is a group of trees, obviously part of an old garden layout: a large Oak, a fine Scots Pine with the cinnamon colour on the upper bark well-developed, and several Ilex trees. From this point one can pass over the bridge which gives access to the walkway to the London Road and the Watermeads. The layout of the Watermeads housing estate caused the death from environmental stress of many fine trees, but a huge Lucombe's Oak, a Cedar of Lebanon and a fine Swamp Cypress remain.

In the remainder of the park, the rarest tree is in the children's playground. This is the Californian Laurel, or Headache Tree, with its yellowish willow-shaped leaves. Nearby is a tree-sized Clerodendrum with white flowers in August/September, followed by blue berries. There are several other plants of the same species in other parts of the park. In the same row is a rare Chinese Cow-tail Pine. This has leaflets arranged flat on each side of the shoot like barbs of a feather. Not far away – near the entrance from Morden Road and the car park – is an ancient Mulberry. In spite of its age it still fruits well.

Amongst smaller plants the most notable are the Giant Rhubarbs and the bamboo clumps near the bridge. The bamboo is not the common species but *Arundinaria simonii*, a taller kind.

With thought for the future the Council have planted new trees of which the most interesting are the Sweet Gums on the south bank of the Wandle. These have maple-like leaves and spectacular autumn colour. Council policy is to maintain both the size and interest of the fine tree plantings inherited from the past, and in time to improve upon them.

River Wandle at Ravensbury Park – postcard c.1930

RAVENSBURY PARK

TREES MENTIONED

Common Name	Botanical Name
London Plane	*Platanus x hispanica*
Common Oak	*Quercus pedunculata*
Black Poplar	*Populus nigra*
Ginkgo	*Ginkgo biloba*
Weymouth Pine	*Pinus strobus*
Swamp Cypress	*Taxodium distichum*
Western Yellow Pine	*Pinus ponderosa*
Indian Bean Tree	*Catalpa bignonioides*
Scots Pine	*Pinus sylvestris*
Ilex (Evergreen Oak)	*Quercus ilex*
Lucombe's Oak	*Quercus lucombeana*
Cedar of Lebanon	*Cedrus libani*
Californian Laurel (Allspice)	*Umbellularia californica*
Clerodendron	*Clerodendrom trichotomum fargesii*
Chinese Cow-tail Pine	*Cephalotaxus fortunei*
Black Mulberry	*Morus nigra*
Sweet Gum	*Liquidambar styraciflua*

J G Berry   1. 9. 80.

Ravensbury Park – postcard postmarked 1954

APPENDIX 3

Memories of the Ravensbury Factory in the 1930s

(Slightly adapted from notes written by Mr Peter Sales, c.1991)

"I knew this area well over the period from 1930 to 1948 when as a child I was a frequent visitor. My grandfather, William Williams, was the bailiff on the Morden Hall Estate and my uncle, Jack Williams, was one of the carpenters. Unfortunately after 1948 my visits were less frequent as in that year I joined the army and was away for long periods for the next 24 years and, after my army service, settled in Shropshire, so my knowledge from then on is sketchy ...

"The 'factory' was used as a warehouse for the Hatfeild estate, it was also the estate workshop. For example – each year one of the haywains was taken out of service, stripped down and rebuilt, and in its 'as new' condition was used as the carriage for the 'May Queen'. This event was held at the recreation ground in Central Road. The vehicle was drawn by two shire horses, their harness polished and their manes be-ribboned. This was the responsibility of their driver, Harry Greenleaf. After this event the vehicle was returned to normal service.

A fragment of the boundary wall of the Ravensbury Print Works,
still to be seen in Ravensbury Park (ENM 1991)

"The waterwheel in the factory was undershot and was in regular use all through the '30s and early '40s. It was used to drive the various machine tools used in the workshop, i.e. drills, planers and saws etc. A sluice gate was opened to allow the water through to drive the wheel and a large lever was used to engage a clutch which transferred the drive to a belt system. The various tools were driven by subsidiary belt systems.

"There were three floors in the building and the main drive went to all three. Each floor had its own system of belt drives, and these were all in place and capable of being used. The top floor was more like an attic right up under the roof. Each of the two upper floors had double doors at one end with hoists for lifting heavy items. Access to each floor inside the building was by shallow open stairways with rope handholds.

"Stored within the building were all the items for daily use on the estate, timber, fencing, bales of wire, glass, doors and frames, sand, cement and other building materials. Smaller items such as door furniture, screws etc, were kept in the 'office' at the house.

"Also stored was all the equipment used for the annual children's parties held in Morden Hall Park. These items were swings, roundabouts, marquees, assorted tents, tables and chairs/benches and the like. Also there were the punts and rowing boats that were used to give the children boats rides on the waterways within the park. This annual event was held over a week or so in the summer when the children from the schools in Mitcham and some of the Morden schools were given a treat of jellies, ice cream, sandwiches, cake, fruit and lemonade, etc. It was something that was looked forward to and remembered all year. Regretfully the outbreak of World War 2 in 1939 and the subsequent death of Mr. Hatfeild put a stop to these wonderful parties and they were never resumed.

"The spillway which ran from the main river by the orchard into the stream by my grandfather's house was brick lined on the sides and the bed was of slate slabs approximately 4 feet by 3 feet by 2 inches thick (they were extremely slippery).

The depth of water from the spillway to where the stream crossed under the road into the park was normally 18 inches to two feet. When the mill was in use it was deeper and faster, as it was when in spate. There were various parts that were deeper, such as where the spillway entered the stream where it was three feet, and at the exit from the tunnel four feet, lessening to 18 inches or so towards the house.

"Within the grounds of the factory there was a 'soakaway' [which had] signs that at one time it had been ornamented as a pool. There were pieces of broken stone which looked at if they had come from decorated slabs, plinths, etc. This, plus a white footbridge, indicated that the pool was not just for practical use.

"Up to the early '40s there were fish in the river and the various streams. They were mainly minnows and three-spined sticklebacks (I used to catch them with a net made from an old stocking, a piece of wire, and a bamboo pole plus, of course, a jam-jar). My grandfather told me that years ago there had been trout in the river. There were also frogs, toads, newts and all the usual water insects, particularly dragonflies. After the '40s all these creatures gradually disappeared due, I assume, to pollution."

Two of the Sales children playing in the Wandle
reproduced by courtesy of Madeline Healey, née Sales

4a: EXCAVATION AT THE GRANGE, MORDEN, 1972
(TQ 2617 6815)

Following the announcement, early in 1972, of a proposal by Messrs. Watney Mann to convert The Grange into a licensed restaurant the Merton Historical Society, Archaeological Section, obtained permission from the Greater London Council to carry out a small-scale exploratory excavation in the grounds. The primary objective was to find evidence of early occupation of the site. Eight trenches were cut, two in the garden, and the remainder near the house. No such evidence was found.

In trenches 5 and 7, to the west of the main building, two sections of 19th-century brick wall were uncovered together with a section of rammed chalk walling of presumably earlier date. These are assumed to be the remains of foundations of previous outbuildings. Trench 6, adjacent to the east veranda, produced a length of brick-built, barrel-topped drain 12 inches by 12 inches internally. Overlying the drain was a scatter of broken tiles, bricks and pottery fragments. The direction of the drain indicated a junction with the south-east corner of the main building, and probably served to carry off waste from a kitchen or wash-house beyond. Above the waste materials was a layer of hard-packed flint which may have been a path or drive, though the latter is not confirmed on map evidence. Whatever its purpose, the drain had collapsed under the superimposed weight and ceased to perform its original function. The drain had 9inch brick sides, a shallow arched top, but no base. It had been cut into the natural clay and partly filled with clay, which would be sufficiently non-absorbent to conduct the water away from the house. The weight above had depressed the arch into the drain leaving no gap. That it had been in use is borne out by the fact

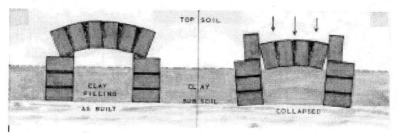

that the clay filling was discoloured at the top. The bricks were red, unevenly fired, had no frogs and were presumably of local manufacture. Specimens were retained.

The pottery recovered, which has not yet been properly classified, is of the 17th and early 18th century, and being roughly contemporary with the first phase of building, was not unexpected. It consists of three main groups. There are a number of sherds of Bellarmine ware, and a small quantity of red glazed earthenware. A handful of tin-glazed earthenware, including a polychrome sherd, was also recovered, with a few sherds of green and yellow glazed white ware. There were some fragments of bottle glass, and iron.

The dense growth of plants, shrubs, etc and a request to reduce clearance to a minimum prevented a more extensive exploration, and in view of the results obtained it was not considered desirable to continue. However, observations will most likely be carried out once the work of conversion has commenced.

Research is at present in progress in an effort to trace the history of The Grange. The early history of the building and the occupants is somewhat obscure. The main building can be described as being of three attached blocks. The oldest, the west block (facing Central Road), is timber-framed and contains re-used timbers of an earlier structure. Where these timbers came from is unknown. A date in the mid to late 17th century has been suggested for the west block, but this is uncertain. Some time later, in the 18th century, a brick-built east block was added. The west block may have been refaced with stucco at the some time. Later still, probably in the 19th century, a north block was built across the end of the other two. The west block has three floors, including an attic. The east and north blocks have two floors, creating split levels. There are considerable extensions to the south, comprising kitchen, pantries, wash-house and dairy.

Report by W J Rudd in Merton Historical Society *Bulletin* 32
(January 1973)

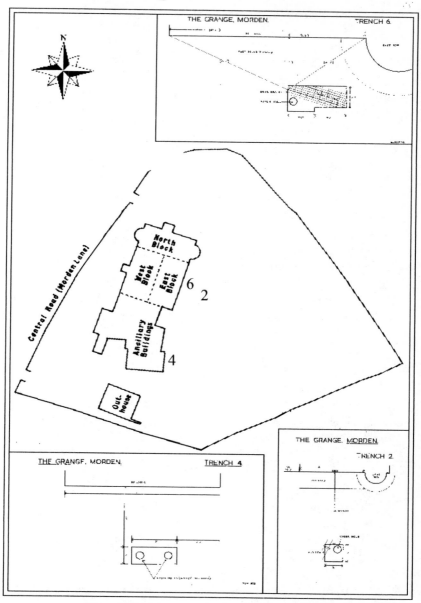

Plan of The Grange, alias Steel Hawes, Morden
with details of three excavation trenches inset (W J Rudd 1972)

THE GRANGE, MORDEN (TQ 2617 6815)

CERAMICS

1 COARSE EARTHENWARES

Red Wares

Milk pans, broken, typically 16" diameter by 2½" high with straight, splayed sides and everted rims, black-flecked glaze in interior only.

Pancheons, broken, typically 1' 6" diameter by 8½" high with near-vertical sides, glazed interior only.

Globular storage jar, broken, 1' 6" diameter with bead rim, glazed interior only.

Sherds of a miscellany of vessels in red or greyish-red ware with varying shades of red and brown glaze. Forms varying – pancheons, pans, lids, breadpots, some with massive loop handles, fragments of a colander, globular jars, etc.

Probably Farnham ware. Late 17th or 18th century.

Off-white Ware

Sherds of shallow pan with interior yellow glaze.

Miscellaneous sherds with yellow or green glaze.

Possibly Surrey ware. Late 17th or 18th century.

Other

One sherd of an olive jar, pink earthenware. Probably Spanish. 17th - 19th century.

Miscellaneous sherds of Staffordshire pressed-ware chargers, decorated with feathered slip, salt-glazed, late 17th or early 18th century.

2 FINE EARTHENWARES

Tin-glaze Delftware

Gallipot, 2" diameter, chipped, but complete. White.

Dinner Plate, 9" diameter, one third complete. Blue on white decoration.

Bowl, 8½" diameter, near complete. Blue on white decoration.

Plates, bowls, chamber pot sherds. Plain white or pale blue.

Plates, miscellaneous sherds. Blue on white decoration. Bowls, ditto.

Probably Lambeth ware. Mid-18th century.

Salt-glaze Whiteware

Sherds from a variety of press-moulded dinner plates, some with basketwork borders, tea bowls and larger bowls with deep foot rings. Staffordshire. Mid-18th century.

Salt-glaze Creamware

Sherds from various sized bowls, typically with deep foot rings.
Dinner plates, shallow dishes and chamber pots; sherds from a variety
of sizes and forms.
Staffordshire. Probably Wedgwood. Second half 18th century.

SMALL FINDS

1 CERAMICS

(a) Coarse Earthenwares

Red Wares

Sherds of pancheons, a bread pot?, and a miscellany of unidentifiable
vessels with varying shades of red and reddish-brown glaze.
Probably Farnham Ware.

Off-White Wares

Sherds of unidentifiable vessels with green, yellow and brown glaze.
Probably Surrey Ware,

Roofing Tile

Pieces of pantiles and plain tiles with peg holes but no nibs.

(b) Fine Earthenwares

Tin-glazed delftware

Small sherds of plates and unidentifiable vessels in white, blue on white
and polychrome.
Probably Lambeth Ware.

Feathered Slipware

A few small sherds.
Probably Staffordshire.

(c) Stonewares

Bellarmine

Sherds of possibly four different flasks, some with medallions.

2 GLASS

A few pieces of thick green bottle glass.

3 METAL

Fragments of nails and other ferrous objects. One fragment of
pewter?

E N Montague (1973)

The finds have been deposited at the London Archaeological Archive and Research Centre

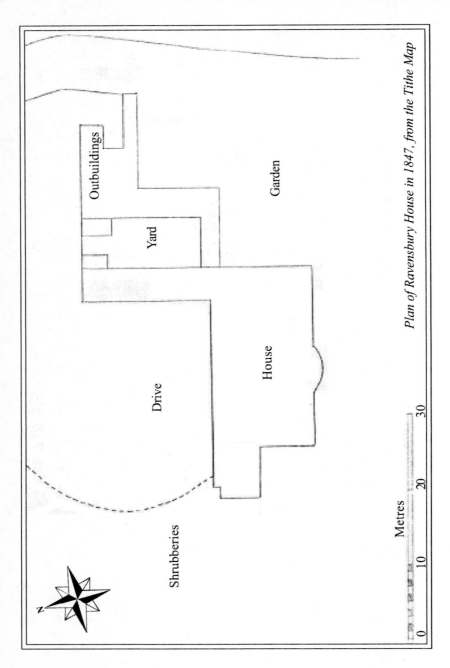

Plan of Ravensbury House in 1847, from the Tithe Map

4b: EXCAVATIONS ON THE SITE OF RAVENSBURY MANOR HOUSE, 1973 (TQ 2665 6804)

In June 1973 an exploratory excavation was conducted by the Society at the invitation of the Borough's Director of Parks and Cemeteries. Three trenches, covering 54 square metres, were opened north-east of the remains of the manor house, exposing a yard surfaced with knapped flint and the site of three domestic outbuildings. One of these was dated to the mid-18th century. All had been demolished by 1867.

Beneath the yard ran an extensive system of brick-built drains, more complex than would appear necessary for domestic use. They pre-dated the flint paving, and were dated on ceramic evidence to the first half of the 18th century. It was evident that these drains were largely disused when the house was enlarged and occupied by John Arbuthnot as his residence in 1755.

The undisturbed soil below the drains, overlying the natural river silt and gravel at 0.7 metres below ground level, contained sherds of coarse black cooking pots and white Surrey ware. The concentration was sufficient, in the small area exposed, to indicate medieval occupation in the vicinity. Fragments of chalk and greensand, both typical building materials of that period and found at the same level, gave support to this theory since they are 'foreign' to this area.

The southern-most trench, exposing footings and other structures associated with a possible scullery or washhouse, also contained a brick-built, cement rendered, rainwater cistern, circular in section and 2 metres deep. This was emptied but found to contain only building rubble and relatively modern glass and stoneware.

The trenches were backfilled after the site had been on view at the end of the excavation.

During the Society's excavation a number of medieval tiles in the park, from Merton Priory, were brought to our notice by the park keeper. The tiles had been cemented under a park bench, by a path that led from the keeper's hut to the river. There were 52 tiles or part tiles altogether. Drawings of the tiles were made and shown to Mrs Elizabeth

Eames of the British Museum who was of the opinion they were of the thirteenth-century Wessex type. This type of tile was found in quite large numbers during excavations at the Priory. Only eight retained their original white or light pink glaze and the patterns, very similar to those already found at the Priory, included pierced 8-foil, fleur-de-lis and part of a griffin. The tiles were probably brought to Ravensbury by Colonel Bidder who excavated part of the Priory in the 1920s and owned the land now making up Ravensbury Park.

E N Montague

Ruins at Ravensbury Manor House on banks of river (ENM June 1967)

4c: EXCAVATIONS AT MITCHAM GROVE, 1974-5
(TQ 271679)

Rescue excavations were arranged in advance of housing development on the site of the known 18th-19th-century house and directed by the writer for Surrey Archaeological Society and Merton Historical Society in July 1974.[1] It was seen as a good site for a training dig but the excavations also had two other aims: locating a Tudor house suggested by documentary evidence and testing the area for any extension of the nearby Anglo-Saxon cemetery.[2]

Geophysical survey was undertaken in May 1974 by a team from the University of Surrey led by Professor Alan Crocker, and succeeded in picking up the exact location of the later house. Trenches for the training excavation could therefore be sited with some precision. As the housing development was delayed, more work was undertaken late in 1974 and early in 1975 in less than ideal circumstances by the John Evelyn Society and Merton Historical Society, with assistance from the newly formed South West London team of Surrey Archaeological Society.[3] Records of work by the latter have not been located. Unfortunately no resources were available for post-excavation work; the project was carried out well before it became the norm for developers to fund archaeological work. As specialist finds reports still need to be completed it is not possible to be precise about the dating of some of the phases but the basic outline is clear.

Five trenches were opened in the first season. One was placed in the nearest available location to test for the Anglo-Saxon cemetery but encountered only modern disturbance. The others all located elements of the later house and the evidence could easily be related to a surviving plan, partly because the foundations of the entrance steps were found. As work continued it could be seen that the front wall of the later building had been created by refronting an earlier structure, probably of Tudor date, and this was in due course shown to have succeeded another building on a different alignment. The later trenching added some details to the plan of the earliest building.

The sequence of events seems to have been as follows. The natural gravel and sand subsoil was succeeded by a layer that was probably in origin agricultural but also represented trample associated with the construction of the medieval building. There were no finds to suggest that this layer was itself pre-medieval, although part of a later Roman bowl and some tile fragments hint at a nearby Roman-period site. There were no prehistoric or Saxon finds. The medieval building was represented by the remains of walls of rough chalk blocks, a cobbled surface and a large amount of tile rubble, in particular one line of tiles resting in the earth over the cobbled surface at an angle to the horizontal – as though they had fallen from a decaying roof and plunged into a damp earth layer overlying the cobbles. This line of tiles was at right angles to the building wall in a different trench, but the wall was found in later testing to have turned away from the tiles (rather than as expected turning to run parallel with them) and so it cannot be said with certainty that they had arrived at their eventual location by falling directly from a roof. The later excavations found a tile-on-edge hearth with greensand block surroundings on roughly the same alignment as the medieval walls and so most probably part of the same building complex. Pottery suggests that the building was constructed in the 12th or 13th century.

The medieval building was robbed of much of its materials, possibly at the same time as the collapse suggested by the line of tiles, and it may have been demolished not long before the Tudor house was constructed, as part of the same programme of work. A different alignment was chosen for this new house, which had chalk block foundations and brick walls. The 'back' wall of this house (assuming that the front was in the same direction as the later building) was not located and it was probably smaller than its successor. At some point in the occupation of the building a sleeper wall was constructed parallel to the front wall and not far behind it, presumably to reinforce floor joists that were rotting where they joined the main wall. Perhaps contemporary with this but more likely later on, the front wall was given a new brick face, based on quarry tiles built along the original wall, with a curving entrance step structure. This 'new' wall was probably matched with a genuinely new build to provide the back wall of the 18th-century house. Internal brick walls and other features were also found, some probably of the same

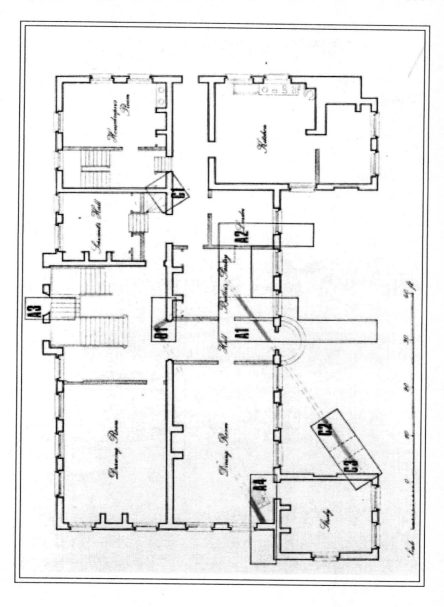

Medieval walls excavated in 1974, superimposed on a copy, drawn by Norman Plastow, of Robert Adam's plan of Mitcham Grove

date as the refronting and others perhaps added later. The whole complex was demolished in due course; an event documented as around 1840. At some point subsequently rubbish apparently derived from pottery making was brought to the site, and there were also spreads of clinker perhaps to be associated with the creation of the cricket ground that had occupied the site until just before excavations began in 1974.

Finds were mostly of pottery and animal bone, representative of occupation across the period from perhaps the 12th century to the 19th. There was little of special note except for a bone shuttle found near the front entrance of the later house, in a post-medieval context. This was at first identified as of Iron Age date, and as such became the basis of a story involving the loss of a find from Wessex, lost by the early archaeologist Colt Hoare while on a visit to Henry Hoare, owner of Mitcham Grove and a relative.[4] Unfortunately for the story, the shuttle is probably to be dated to the post-medieval period[5] and thus matches its context on site (although of course this does not detract from the general point that Clive Orton was making). One aspect of post-excavation work that is still needed is a specialist report on the material related to pottery manufacture found in later levels on the site in the hope that this can explain its presence. It is unlikely to relate to local manufacture and its origin would therefore be of interest.

D G Bird

Mitcham Grove excavations 1974 – entrance portico from southeast

Abbreviations

Bidder and Morris	Bidder H F, and Morris J, 'The Anglo-Saxon Cemetery at Mitcham' in *SyAC* LVI (1959)
BL	British Library
Braithwaite	Braithwaite F, 'On the Rise and Fall of the River Wandle' *Proceedings of the Institution of Civil Engineers* 20 (1861)
Brayley	Brayley E W, *Topographical History of Surrey*
DNB	*Dictionary of National Biography*
Edwards	Edwards J, *Companion from London to Brighthelmston*
Gover *et al*	Gover J E B, Mawer M, and Stenton F M, *The Place Names of Surrey* English Place Names Society XI (1934)
Heales	Heales A, *The Records of Merton Priory* (1898)
LMA	London Metropolitan Archives
Lysons	Lysons D, *Environs of London*
McGow	McGow P, *Notes on the Mills of the Wandle*, transcript deposited at the Wandle Industrial Museum, can be consulted at http://www.wandle.org
Manning & Bray	Manning O, and Bray W, *History and Antiquities of Surrey*
MHS	Merton Historical Society
Michell	Michell R, *The Carews of Beddington* (1981)
Minet	Lambeth Archives, Minet Library
Mitcham Tithe	Mitcham Tithe Apportionment 1846/7 – original map and register at SHC, photocopies at MLSC, published by MHS as *Local History Notes 22* (2002)
MLSC	Merton Local Studies Centre
Montgomery	Montgomery, F M, *Printed Textiles. English and American Cottons and Linens 1700-1850* (1970)
Morden Tithe	Morden Tithe Apportionment 1837/8 – original map and register at SHC, photocopies at MLSC, published by MHS as *Local History Notes 13* (1998)
NGR	National Grid Reference
Prentis	Prentis W H, *The Snuff Mill Story* (1970)
Reliquary	Rice, R. Garroway, 'On the Parish Registers of Ss. Peter and Paul, Mitcham' *The Reliquary* 1877
SHC	Surrey History Centre
Slater	Slater, B, 'Reminiscences of Old Mitcham' in Bidder H F (Editor) *Old Mitcham* (1923)
SyRS	Surrey Record Society
SyAC	*Surrey Archaeological Collections*
TNA	The National Archives
VCH	*Victoria County History of Surrey*
WAM	Westminster Abbey Muniments

1   THE MANOR OF RAVENSBURY

Note: Hone N J, *The Manor and Manorial Records* (1906) 281:

"Mitcham (Ravensbury) Various dates, 1488-1642" in the "British Museum MS Dept." [but now in the British Library] – Cf. *Catalogue of Charters and Rolls* (1901) printed by the Trustees of the British Museum.

――――

Origins

1   After noting that the manor of Ravensbury was held of the lords of Ashtead manor, the *VCH* IV (1912) 232 suggested that "As Ashtead, like Mitcham and Witford, was held by the canons of Bayeux of the Bishop in 1086, it is possible that here too we have part of the canons' holding, granted with Ashtead to the Mara family".

Brayley IV (1841) 89 expressed the opinion that Lank's pre-Conquest holding, which was incorporated post-1066 in Fitz Ansculf's Witford estate, became Ravensbury manor. It can now be demonstrated to have become part of the manor of Ravensbury.

2   Gover *et al*, 52 list

Wicford	1199 FF(p)
Wikeford(e)	1200 cur 1219 FF 1241 Ass
Wikford	1229 FF
Wycford	1242 Fees(p)
Wickford	1279 Ass
Wykford	*c*.1280 BL

The form 'Witford' seems to have been a creation of the compilers of Domesday Book, with an h being added by 18th/19th century translators to give 'Whitford'

3   SHC 212/113

4   Morris J & Wood S (ed), *Domesday Book – Surrey* (1975) 21,1

5   Burns D, *The Sheriffs of Surrey* (1992) 3

6   Manning & Bray I (1804)

7   See Appendix 4b

8   Manning & Bray II (1809) 499, quoting Testa de Nevil.

9   Lysons I (1792) 351, quoting Harleian MSS, BL No. 313. f.15, and Manning & Bray II (1809) 499

A 'knight's fee' was a form of feudal tenure obliging the holder in theory to provide a fully armed knight and his servants for 40 days a year. Often commuted to a money payment.

10   Historical Manuscript Commission. *Report on the MSS of Lord Middleton* (1911), then at Wollaton Hall, and subsequently Notts. Record Office, quoted by John Blair, of The Queen's College, Oxford, in a personal communication to the writer.

See also Meekings C A F, *The 1235 Surrey Eyre* (SyRS XXXI 1979) 218: It is here stated that Ralph received Ravensbury from "Rabel the Chamberlain before 1140".

11　I am indebted to Lionel Green (personal communication dated 9 September 1994) for biographical information on de Tancarville, Ralph fitz Robert, and Mary of Ashtead.

12　Middleton, *op. cit.*, Sir Christopher Hatton's Book of Seals 72 and College of Arms Vincent MS 46 (also quoted by John Blair in personal communication)

13　Gover *et al*, 53

14　BL MS Add. 6040 f.1 No.1. Transcribed by John Blair.

15　BL MS Add. 6040 f.1 No.2. Transcribed by John Blair.

16　*VCH* IV (1912) 233, quoting *VCH* I 231

17　*VCH* IV (1912) 233, quoting Feet of Fines Surr. 3 Hen. III, no.23

18　BL MS Add. 6040 f.2 No.20. Transcribed by John Blair.

19　*VCH* IV (1912) 233, quoting Ancient Deed (TNA) A 9189

To 'enfeoff' was to put a tenant legally in possession of a holding.

The de Mara Dynasty

1　Malden H E, 'Ashtead and the de Mara Chantry' *SyAC* XIX (1906)

2　Milward R, *Early Wimbledon* (1969) 30-31 and *Historic Wimbledon* (1989) 91 states that in the 13th century the "de la Mares ran the mill". The de la Mares themselves are hardly likely to have been directly involved in the actual running of the mill, as this implies, and can be assumed to have held the mill on a lease, sub-leasing it to a miller.

3　Burns D, *The Sheriffs of Surrey* (1992) 8

4　Heales 86 and Jowett E M, *A History of Merton and Morden* (1951) 31

5　D J Turner, in *SyAC* LXVI (1969) 114

6　Meekings C A F, *The 1235 Surrey Eyre* (SyRS XXXI) 220

7　Manning & Bray II (1809) 499 quoting Cotton MSS. BM [now BL] Cleopatra, C.VII. f.111, 112

VCH IV (1912) 232 also quoting [BL] Cott. MS. Cleop. vii.

8　Gover *et al*, 53

9　Heales, 110-111

10　Lysons I (1792) 353, and Manning & Bray II (1809) 499, quoting Cart. 11 Edw I. No. 24, whereas

VCH IV (1912) 232, quoting Cal. Chart. R. 1257-1300, p.267, gives her name as "Parnel", the diminutive of Petronilla, and the surname as "de la Mare".

11　*VCH* IV (1912) 232 says the manor was referred to as "Ersbourne" in the inquisition, but also uses the forms "Ersboury" and "Rasebury".

Manning & Bray II (1809) 499, quoting the date 7 Edw. II 1314, call the manor "Ersborn in Micham", but question this. *VCH* IV 232 refers to the deceased as "William" de la Mare.

12 Manning & Bray II (1809) 499 and *Victoria County History of Northamptonshire* I 291

The "property outside the manor" could well have been 'Jenkingranger' (on the site of the later Colliers Wood House), to which we shall refer later.

13 Heales 189

14 SHC 212/113

15 Manning & Bray II (1809) 499 quoting Esc. 7 Edw. II. no. 20. Lodelowe held the land "of the heirs of William de Marisco in capite".

16 *VCH* IV (1912), 232, quoting Cal. Inq. p.m. 1-9 Edw. II, 250

17 Peter de Montfort married Maud de la Mare, granddaughter of William de la Mare, after the death of her father Henry in 1256. Meekings C A F, *The 1235 Surrey Eyre* (SyRS XXXI) 220

18 Lewis F B, 'Pedes Finium' 87 11 Ed. II in *Surrey Archaeological Society Extra Volume* I (1894) 233

19 *VCH* IV (1912) 232 quoting Feet of Fines Surr, 14 Edw. II, no. 27

20 *VCH* IV (1912) 232 quoting 2 Edw. III, no. 23

21 *VCH* IV (1912) 232 quoting 21 Edw. III, no. 35

A 'quit claim' is a release and disclaimer of all rights, interest and potential legal actions from a grantor to a grantee.

22 *VCH* IV (1912) 232 quoting Feet of F. Surr, 21 Edw. III, no. 9

23 *VCH* IV (1912) 233 quoting Ancient Deed (TNA) A 5695

24 *VCH* IV (1912) 232 quoting (TNA) A 4012

25 From "de la Mare", "de la Mar", and "de Mara" of the 12th–13th centuries, we now begin to encounter "Mareys", and "Mares" as derivative forms of the same name.

26 *Surrey Taxation Returns – Fifteenths and Tenths Part (A) The 1332 Assessment* SyRS No. XVIII (1922) 61

27 *Calendar of Close Rolls* X (1908) 308/9

28 *Calendar of Close Rolls* Ibid, Edw. III XI 302. "Sir" [*dominus*] was a title, commonly applied to clerics. *VCH* IV 233 gives no names, and merely refers to "the vicars", whilst Manning and Bray II 499, quoting Claus. 35 Edw. III. m.3, dors, give a slightly different rendering and only mention "Richard Porter and others".

29 Dom S F Hockey (ed) *The Register of William Edington Bishop of Winchester 1346-1366* Hampshire Record Series VII & VIII (1986, 1987), entry 1261

30 *VCH* IV (1912) 233, quoting Inq. a.q.d. 395, no. 28

31 *VCH* IV (1912) 233, quoting Valor. Eccl. (Rec. Com.), ii, 48

32 McKisack M, *The Fourteenth Century 1307-1399* (1963) 324

Ravensbury – Medieval Real-Estate

1   *VCH* IV (1912) 232, quoting Feet of Fines Surr. 1 Ric. II, no. 4

2   *VCH* IV (1912) 232, quoting Feet of Fines Surr. 5 Ric. II, no. 5

3 *VCH* IV (1912) 232, quoting Anct. D. (TNA) B 2608

4 Jones A E, *An Illustrated Directory of Old Carshalton* (1973) 203.

5 SHC 599/ – Coombs W W, 'A Calendar of Deeds Relating to Mitcham'

6 Manning & Bray II (1809) 505 quoting Esc. 15 R.II. n.8

7 A John Arundel, Governor of Southampton, successfully repelled an attack on the port by French transports, but lost an invasion fleet bound for Brittany in an Atlantic storm during the winter of 1379. It is not known if this was the same John Arundel who married Lady Grenville.

8 *VCH* IV (1912) 232 says 672 acres

9 Manning & Bray II (1809) 505, apparently quoting Esc. 2 Hen. VI n. 29

10 'Allmannesland' is now occupied by the house and grounds known as Park Place, 54 Commonside West

11 *VCH* IV (1912) 232

12 SHC 320/1/13

13 *VCH* IV (1912) 232 quoting Pat. 3 Hen. VII, pt. ii, m.4
    A holding 'in tail' is one that cannot be bequeathed at pleasure, i.e. it is inalienable.

14 Manning & Bray II (1809) 499

15 Lysons I (1792) 353 quoting Cotton. Cart. Antiq. BL xii. 24

Ravensbury and the Carews

1 *VCH* IV (1912) 231, quoting Pat. 36 Hen. VIII pt. xxvii

2 *VCH* IV (1912) 232, quoting Chanc, Proc. Hh, 17 Eliz. no.3; see also Pat. 30 Eliz. pt.vi, m.14, and Pat. 2. & 3 Phil. and Mary pt.iv, m.36

3 SHC K77/4/1. Information kindly supplied by Peter Hopkins in 1999

4 SHC 470 – James Cranmer's Rent and Memorandum Book of Mitcham 1717-1740

5 SHC 320/2/1 – Plans of Several Estates within the Manor of Ravensbury 1825

6 *SyAC* XIX (1906) 42

7 *DNB* XIX 807-814

8 Michell 67 & 76-8. See also SHC 2163/6/7 - an undated document of the 17th century showing the annual income of Nicholas Carew from his manors

9 BL *Catalogue of Charters and Rolls* (1901) 281, listed by Hone N J, *The Manor and Manorial Records* (1906) 243

10 Transferred from F R Allen & Co, 3 Clements Inn, WC2 to SHC at the writer's suggestion

The End of the Manor

1 Michell 110

2 SHC – Deeds of Chestnut Cottage, Mitcham Cricket Green

3 *VCH* IV (1912) 232

2 RAVENSBURY MANOR HOUSE

The Ruins

1 NGR TQ 2665 6804

2 Prentis 98

The Early Years – The Carews and the Garths

3 The excavation, under the direction of the author, was carried out by students of Rowan Girls' School, at the invitation of the Deputy Director of Parks, James Berry. See Appendix 4b and *SyAC* LXXXI (1977) 286-7

4 London County Council, *Court Minutes of the Surrey and Kent Sewer Commission* (1909) 120

5 *SyAC* XIX (1906) 42

6 *DNB* XIX 807-814

7 *The Visitations of Surrey 1623* Harleian Society (1899), and information from W Rudd in a personal communication.

8 *Surrey Hearth Tax 1664* SyRS XVII

9 SHC 212/9/2

10 Woodhead J R, *The Rulers of London 1660-1689* (1965) 83

11 The inscription reads "Here lyes interred the body of Henry Hampson, merchant, son of Henry Hampson Esq, and Ann his wife who departed this life the 15th March 1691 aged 48".

The entry in the parish register (SHC) describes him as "Henry Hampson the 2^d" and adds that he was buried in wool 28 March 1691.

12 Information from W Rudd in a personal communication

The Arbuthnots of Ravensbury

13 MLSC – Mitcham Vestry Minutes 1807-1823 196

14 Lambeth Archives (Minet Library) – Calendar of Surrey Deeds No. 3380

15 Tombs in Morden churchyard

16 *VCH* II (1905) 374

17 *DNB* I (1922)

18 MHS *Bulletin* 141 (March 2002) 4; MHS *Bulletin* 142 (June 2002) 11

19 SHC K85/2/42

20 The admiral's name first appears in the Land Tax records as 'The Proprietor', i.e. tax payer, in 1780, but the books reflect changes taking place the previous year.

21 Edwards II (1789) 18

22 *DNB* I (1922) 537-8

23 SHC – Morden Land Tax records

24 Caption to a print on display in Buckler's Hard museum. In a personal communication A J Holland, former curator of Buckler's Hard Museum, questioned the accuracy of this caption.

The Last Years of the Old Manor House: 1800–*c*. 1860

25 SHC – Mitcham Land Tax records

A plan of part of the Wandle flowing through the estate of Richard Carew, produced by W Lazonby after a survey in 1804 and now Minet 62/1804, describes Carew as of "Raven Berry House".

26 Information in a letter to the Hon Secretary of MHS from John E Barnard of Temple Guiting, Cheltenham, in April 1992

27 Information in a personal communication from Mrs Marian P Sartin of Harrow (family history researcher) in October 1991

28 The career of the Hon Sir Hugh Arbuthnot KGB of Hatton-Bervie (second son of the 7th Viscount Arbuthnot) is outlined in Clarke S, *Cameron Highlanders* (1913) 136

29 Greenwood C & J, *Surrey Described* (1823) 233

30 Seen when in the possession of J Turner, Devonshire Road, Sutton

31 MLSC Extra-Illustrated copy of Brayley E W *History of Surrey* III

32 Croydon Local Studies Library HW 904 and London Borough of Sutton Archives 2361/2/2 – Sale particulars of Henry Hoare's estate, 1828

33 *SyAC* LXVII (1970) 55-59

34 Braithwaite 200

35 SHC K85/4/95

36 SHC K85/590-601

37 'G.O.M. of Mitcham – As Charter Mayor' (R.M Chart's memories) *Mitcham Mercury Charter Day Souvenir* 21 September 1934, 3

Ravensbury and The Bidders

38 For much of the information that follows on the Bidder family I am indebted to

(1) E F Clark, great-great-grandson of George Parker Bidder, author of *George Parker Bidder, The Calculating Boy* (1983), with whom I exchanged correspondence between 1978 and 1980
(2) Critical correspondence from George Parker Bidder III and Col Harold F Bidder printed in the *Mitcham Advertiser* following publication of an article 'Famous Sons of Mitcham' on 6 November 1924
(3) *DNB* II (1921-2) 474-5
(4) *Mitcham Advertiser* 5 April 1968. Obituary on Col Harold F Bidder by Evelyn Jowett

39 On its course from Mitcham Station to Croydon the railway followed the route formerly taken by the Surrey Iron Railway.

40 E F Clark believes that Ravensbury Park was designed by (Sir) Henry Arthur Hunt (1810-1889), who was a partner in the firm of Hunt, Stephenson & Jones of 45 Parliament Street, Westminster. By profession a surveyor, he was surveyor to the fabric of Westminster Abbey.

41 'The Lesser Country Houses of Today: Ravensbury Manor, Mitcham' *Country Life* 8 March 1913, 7–

42 MLSC – Urban District Council Minutes and file of cuttings

43 Prentis 123-4

3   RAVENSBURY FARM

1   SHC K80/5/90-91
2   SHC 2065/4/31 – Morden Poor Law records
3   SHC K80/5/85; K80/5/100
4   Information from W J Rudd
5   SHC 2065/4/42 – Morden Poor Law records
6   SHC K85/4/68
7   Letter to W J Rudd from Grace Minter's son, D L Minter, in April 1972, when Mr Minter lived in Pollard Road, Morden, now in the file on The Grange deposited by MHS with Museum of London – GGM72.
8   Undated newspaper cutting, now in the file on The Grange deposited with Museum of London – GGM72.
9   Grade III scheduled building on the Supplementary List of the Ministry of Housing and Local Government
10 Undated newspaper cutting, now in the file on The Grange deposited with Museum of London – GGM72.
11 Now in the file on The Grange deposited with Museum of London – GGM72.
12 Copies of Photographic Unit, Department of Architecture and Civic Design, Greater London Council, ref 66/8066, 66/8068, and 66/8070 are in the file on The Grange deposited with Museum of London – GGM72.
13 The beams were trimmed and preserved and incorporated into the replica building, but they are no longer load-bearing
14 Undated report by A Quiney, Department of Architecture and Civic Design, Greater London Council. A copy was supplied to Merton Historical Society in February 1972, and annotated copies are in the file on The Grange deposited with Museum of London – GGM72. The section covering the early occupation of the building is not reliable.
15 The finds, site notes and other documentation have been deposited with the Museum of London's London Archaeological Archive & Research Centre – GGM72.
16 C and I Greenwood *Surrey Described* (1823) p232
17 Minet 3423/1, /2, /4, /5
18 Minet 3423/1, /2, /4, /5
19 Minet 3423/2
20 Minet 3423/3
21 SHC 2065/4/35-45 – Morden Poor Law records
22 SHC K80/5/90-91
23 Minet 3423/1, /2, /4, /5
24 SHC 2065/4/6 – Morden Poor Law records
25 SHC 2065/4/5 – Morden Poor Law records
26 SHC 2065/4/3-4 – Morden Poor Law records
27 SHC 2065/4/1 – Morden Poor Law records

28 London Borough of Sutton Archives 2361/2/2, 2361/2/6

29 SHC 2065/4/1 – Morden Poor Law records

30 Minet 3380 – The 37 acres are described in the 1764 lease as:

"all that field adjoining on the west of lands of John Arbuthnot	10 acres
and all that other field thereto adjoining	6 acres
two fields adjoining on lands of John Arbuthnot	
and south on Mitcham River	18 acres
all that wood coppice and Shaw and Ruff Lane	
adjoining on Edwards Lane and the River	3 acres
in Morden, late in the tenure of Thomas Stacey	
and now of John Arbuthnot"	

Fieldnames in the 1828 Hoare sales particulars and the 1838 tithe apportionment suggest that these 37 acres were tithe ref. 311, 313-4, part of 315, 316-7, 319-320. In 1838 plot 311 was the site of the farm and barn, not mentioned in the lease – they had presumably been built by Arbuthnot.

31 SHC 2065/4/1 – Morden Poor Law records; Morden Land Tax records (on microfilm)

32 London Borough of Sutton Archives 2361/2/2, 2361/2/6

33 A H Smith *English Place-Name Elements* English Place-Name Society 25, 26 (1956) p150

34 Morden Tithe – ref 353

35 SHC K85/2/13 [4]; K85/3/28 pp18-20;

36 SHC K85/2/6-8

37 SHC K85/2/12

38 TNA A4/4 fo.232 (transcribed by John Wallace); SHC K85/2/18

39 SHC K85/2/19

40 SHC G1/1/50a; K2575/3/G; TNA A4/9 fo.68; A4/12 fo.11

41 SHC K85/2/79-80

42 SHC K85/2/51-52

43 SHC K85/2/79

44 SHC K85/2/79

45 SHC K85/2/80

46 SHC K85/2/80

47 Minet 5860

48 SHC K85/2/80

49 SHC K85/2/81

50 Morden Tithe – ref 326-7, 333-4

51 Morden Tithe – ref 337-8, 343-8

52 Morden Tithe – ref 330-332

53 SHC K85/1/3

54 SHC K80/5/62; K85/4/1-11

55 SHC K80/5/42, 44, 46

56 Article on Bazalgette by W J Rudd in MHS *Bulletin* 142 (June 2002) p2

57 Feet of Fines Surrey 14 Edw II, no.27 (*SyAC Extra Volume* 1 (1894))

4   RAVENSBURY PRINT WORKS

1   7 acres called 'Flemynge mede' are listed among the demesne lands of Merton Priory, leased to Sir Thomas Hennage, in Ministers Accounts of 1538 – TNA SC 6/HEN VIII/3463; another 4 acres 'portion or parcel of meadow late in the occupation of William Pratte, lying and being in a certain meadow of ours called Flemymede in Mycham' were among the lands granted to Robert Wylforde in 1544. Hennage's holding is specifically excluded from this grant – SHC 599/219

2   'The Lay Subsidy Assessments for the County of Surrey in 1593 or 1594', *SyAC* XVIII (1906)

3   SHC – Mitcham Parish Registers

4   Croydon Local Studies Library. Ms note by Garroway Rice

This discovery was subsequently published in the *Proceedings of the Croydon Natural History and Scientific Society* LXXVII (1917-18).

The stone is said to have resembled Kimmeridge Shale, and to have had on the edge, in well-cut black letters, part of an inscription in Flemish which read "... Pauline, his first wife, was in the year 1527 ...".

5   SHC – Surrey Quarter Sessions Records

6   A bored elm trunk was discovered here in 1962

Turner D J, 'Wooden Water Pipe at Ravensbury Park, Mitcham' in *SyAC* LXVII (1970) 55-59

7   Montgomery 16

8   Quoted by Montgomery 15

9   Turnbull G, *A History of the Calico Printing Industry of Great Britain* (1951) 21

10   Mauvillain papers kept by Barclays Bank. (Quoted by W Rudd in correspondence)

11   SHC K85/2/12 and 36

In a bargain and sale of 7 March 1553/4 the "Newly built mansion house called Growtes", copyhold, plus the copyhold land of Stelehawes, was sold by Edward Whitchurch, citizen and haberdasher of London, to Richard Garth of London, gent. (K85/2/12).

It was sold again in 1682, by Jane Garth, widow, to William Booth. An undated endorsement to the deed of sale, in an 18th-century hand, describes the property as "A house that Mavillain bought that Selby lives in." (K85/2/36).

12   MLSC

13   SHC 683/1

14   SHC K85/2/51-52

15   Lysons I (1792) 363

In 1681 Francis Mauvillain, a French Protestant refugee from Cozes, in Saintonge, in the Department of Charente-Inf, was granted a letter of denization, usually a preliminary to naturalisation. Peter Mauvillain, who was presumably his son, appears in the denization and naturalisation records of 1688 and 1689, apparently taking the oath on attaining his majority. He, it seems likely, is the Peter Mauvillain who lies beside his wife Sarah in Morden parish churchyard.

(Information from Joyce Wheatley, Research Assistant, Huguenot Society)

Peter and Sarah's monument, triangular in section and surmounted by an escarbuncle, bears arms described as Goutee a pile, charged with three Cinquefoils. Peter died 31 May 1739, aged 72, and Sarah two years later. Stephen Mauvillain was survived by his wife Hannah and their two daughters, Hannah and Sarah, the former marrying into the Stone family at Tooting in 1743. Sarah died unmarried. Both sisters are buried in the north aisle of Westminster Abbey, near the grave of Hannah's husband Andrew, a distinguished academician, who attained high office under George III. (Information supplied by William J Rudd, being extracts from Joseph Lemuel Chester's *Transcriptions of the Marriage and Baptismal Registers of the Collegiate Church or Abbey of St Peter, Westminster* (1876)).

16   SHC K85/2/151

17   SHC K85/4/95

18   *VCH* II (1905) 374

"It is not improbable that the Ravensbury printing works were started by Mr. John Cecil of Ravensbury, Mitcham, who was buried at Morden 21 April 1760. Mr. John Cecil apparently came from the Merton Abbey works, for it is stated in the monumental inscription to Mrs. Hannah Cecil in Morden churchyard that 'she died at Merton Abbey near this parish, January the 3rd. 1756, aged 58 years'."

In view of what now seems to be the history of the Ravensbury works, the above supposition is clearly questionable. A more likely explanation is that after the death of his wife, John Cecil left Merton Abbey to take up residence at Ravensbury Manor House with his daughter and son-in-law. He may, of course, have assisted Arbuthnot financially at the outset.

19   SHC P40/1 – Mitcham Poor Rate Books

The vestry minutes show Whapham taking a responsible part in parish affairs in the mid-18th century, serving as churchwarden, overseer of the poor and surveyor of highways.

20   SHC K85/4/95

21   Montgomery 13/14

22   SHC Deeds, Ravensbury.

23   SHC – Land Tax Records, Mitcham

24 Edwards II (1789) 18
25 *VCH* II (1905) 374
26 Royal Exchange Fire Insurance Policy 120664 24 March 1791

The agent appears to have been Sarah Benton of Mitcham, who also ran a bakery business.

27 *Ambulator or a Pocket Companion in a Tour Round Londo*n ed. 5 (1793) 260 (quoted by *VCH* II, 373) and (1794) 185

Malcolm J, *A Compendium of Modern Husbandry* (1805) refers to the Wandle serving Mr Fenning's calico and printing grounds, and a plan of the Wandle through the estate of Richard Carew, drawn by W Lazonby in 1804 (Minet 64/180) gives details of Fenning's works.

28 *VCH* II (1905) 374

The *Gentleman's Magazine*, reporting Fenning senior's death, describes him "of Ravensbury grounds. Mitcham" – the "grounds" being the bleaching or whitening grounds which at this time played a vital role in the preparation of calico for printing.

29 TNA WO 13 4060 – Muster Lists
30 SHC K80/4/43
31 His will, in which he is described as a calico printer, suggests that the bleaching and printing of calico, as opposed to other textiles, still formed the main, if not sole, activities at Ravensbury.
32 Pigot's *Directory*, 1826-7 and Land Tax records
33 Here again, the compilers of *VCH* were not entirely correct when they stated "From this time" (1823) "the works gradually dwindled in importance, and ceased towards the middle of the century". *VCH* II, 374
34 SHC – Morden Land Tax records, and Register of Electors
35 SHC K80/4/44

Fixtures, machinery and utensils were included in this lease, as well as buildings – See schedule K85/4/89.

36 Clarke S, *Cameron Highlanders* (1913) 136.
37 SHC – Book of Reference d/d 29.11.1836, listing occupiers of mills on the Wandle QS 6/8/164
38 SHC K85/4/88
39 SHC K85/4/89

The mortgagees were the Child family. The mortgage document describes in great detail the contents of the numerous parts of the factory.

40 Pigot, *Directory of Surrey* (1839)
41 Wallington Library. Notes by the Revd H G Dodd in which he states that many of the 'Paisley shawls' popular in Victorian times were made by the Mitcham firm of Walmesley. The local illustrations collection includes a faded photograph of a lady wearing one of these shawls.
42 MLSC – The Revd. Herbert Randolph's Notebook 1837/38, published by MHS as Local History Notes 20 (2002)
43 TNA – Census 1841 – Mitcham

44 SHC K85/4/89
45 McGow citing *London Gazette*, 21 February 1845
46 McGow citing *London Gazette*, 31 May 1850
47 MLSC – Copy Tithe Register and Map

Ref.	1179	Meadow
	1180	Farm Yard and buildings
	1182	Bleaching ground and building
	1185	Houses, gardens
	1186	Printing Factory etc.
	1181	House and garden

Total: 14 acres 1 rood 23 perches

Landowner: Captain Charles Hallowell Carew

Occupier: John Geary, dyer

48 SHC K85/4/97
49 Slater
50 Braithwaite 200-201
51 SHC K85/4/95

The sale particulars of 1855 (K80/5/90) contain a description of the dwelling house, cottage etc and yards.

52 McGow citing *London Gazette*, 15 April 1856
53 SHC K85/4/100 and 101

The history of the final 20 years of the Ravensbury factory, during which various, but unsuccessful, attempts were made to find a viable use for the premises, is well documented by the Hatfeild estate papers held by the SHC. Amongst this collection are a number of interesting notices of sale, and also contemporary plans of the works.

54 SHC K85/4/102-104

William Simpson was the son of William Simpson of Litchfield, a former partner in calico printing firms at Merton Abbey and Carshalton, who became the 'squire' of Mitcham. He died in 1860.

55 SHC K85/4/107
56 Revd D F Wilson's Annual Letter and Report 1860
57 SHC K85/4/110 and 112
58 SHC K85/4/113
59 SHC K85/4/114/115
60 SHC K85/4/120
61 SHC K85/4/121
62 SHC K85/4/122-124
63 SHC 6159/5/1-20
64 Information from his granddaughter, Madeline Healey

5 THE RAVENSBURY SNUFF MILLS

1 One of the Mitcham mills may be identifiable with Wickford, or Mitcham, Mill, located above Mitcham Bridge, whilst the other can be placed, albeit tentatively, in the vicinity of Phipps Bridge, where there was a mill in the 13th century. The site of the Morden mill has not been identified, but the late Evelyn Jowett believed it would have been on the Wandle. If so, the Morden Hall snuff mills provide a possible location.

2 Milward R, *Early Wimbledon* (1969) 31 and *Historic Wimbledon* (1989) 91

3 SHC 212/9/2 – Rent rolls of the manors of Bandon, Norbury and Ravensbury

4 Michell 84

5 Mitcham Tithe – £3 4s 0d paid to the vicar and £3 19s 0d to William and Emily Simpson

6 The present mill head may date from this period also. From the evidence of the boundary between the parishes of Mitcham and Morden it does not appear, however, that at Ravensbury the Wandle was diverted from its former course, which contrasts with the extensive works carried out downstream to serve the snuff mills in Morden Hall Park.

7 MLSC

8 SHC LA5/4/1

9 SHC LA5/4/2

10 London Guildhall Library

11 SHC LA5/4/6 and LA5/4/9

12 For information on the poor rate and land tax records of Morden I am indebted to an unpublished thesis on Ravensbury Mill written in about 1970 by the late Miss Winifred A Mould (a fellow member of MHS).

13 Prentis 90-1

14 Edwards (1789)

15 Seen when in the possession of John Turner, Devonshire Road, Sutton

16 Prentis 86

17 McGow

18 Guildhall Library Vols 369, 379 & 387 – Sun Fire Insurance Policies Nos. 573544 (1790); 588589 (1791) and 604906 (1792)

19 Michell 105

20 Thomas, T, *Ravensbury Mill. An Archaeological Evaluation* (1992)

21 Mould, W A, *op. cit.*

22 Edwards II (1801) 18

23 Minet drawing 62/1804

24 Probate 11/1695

25 Edwards II (1801) 28

26 Peter Hopkins in pers. comm. quoting SHC K85/2/151-156

27 Pigot's *Directories* 1824/5 and 1839

28   SHC – Book of Reference dated 29 Nov 1834 listing occupiers of mills, etc.

     SHC QS 6/8/124 – Premises on the site of the Ravensbury Mills (Reference No.3) are described as "Snuff Mill", owned by Sir Benjamin Hallowell Carew's executors, leased and occupied by Isaac Rutter.

     The land held by the Rutters is shown on the Morden tithe map and listed in the register.

29   *Post Office Directory* 1845. "Rutter, John and Isaac, tobacco and snuff manufacturers, Ravensbury Mills."

30   George Park Bidder's diary – information from E F Clark (Bidder's great-great-grandson) in a personal communication, February 1978

     Isaac Campbell Rutter, a former churchwarden and overseer at Mitcham, died in 1887, and is commemorated in the parish church by the reredos, donated by his relatives in 1891.

31   Braithwaite 201

32   Mitcham Tithe – plots 1137, 1157, 1159 & 1160 (Meadow); 1161 (Gardens); 1163 (Barn and Yard); 1183 (Buildings and Yard); 1162 (Cottage and Yard) and 1167 (Gardens).

33   SHC K85/4/148-156

     Also *Kelly's Directories* 1874-78

     The register of St Lawrence Morden records the burials of three children of William Edward Lewis and Constance Hooper between 1878 and 1880. Each died within a few hours of birth.

34   *Kelly's Directory* 1925 etc.

35   For an excellent description of Whitely's and their products, see Festing S, 'Ravensbury Mills – A local industry' *Merton Borough News* Summer 1973.

36   Prentis 89, contains a detailed description of the machinery visible inside the mill in the late 1960s

37   NGR TQ 2640 6817. London Borough of Merton: List of Buildings of Special Architectural or Historic Interest, November 1990

6   WHITE COTTAGE, MORDEN ROAD, MITCHAM.

1   Both names may be relatively recent, and appear not to have been current before the beginning of the 20th century. It was also known as 'Ravenspring', and in Gilliat Edward Hatfeild's will of 1941 it was called 'The White House'.

2   Edwards (1789)

3   SHC – Mitcham Land Tax records

     MLSC – 1841 Census returns and Mitcham Tithe

4   SHC K85/4/318

5   SHC K85/4/320

6   SHC – Catalogue of Hatfeild deeds K85/4/-

7   This map was on display in Morden Hall in the late 1940s, but was later moved to the National Trust office at the snuff mills.

8   SHC – Certificate of Contract for Redemption of Land Tax No. 66729 d/d 16.2.88.

9   SHC K85/4/313

10 MLSC – Tom Francis lecture notes 76 166

11 NGR TQ 26 NE 4/105 33rd List dated 2 September 1988

7   MITCHAM GROVE

The General Picture

1   Edwards II (1801) 18

Hassell J, *Picturesque Rides and Walks I* (1817) 117/8

Brayley E W, (Edit) *The Ambulator* [various editions, including the 12th (1819)] 225

Pigot and Co's *Directory* 1826/7 and

Greenwood C & J, *Surrey Described* (1823) 120

2   Under the direction of David Bird, Surrey County Archaeological Officer. See Appendix 4c

3   Manning & Bray II (1809) 490 quoting Claus. 35 Edw. III m.3 and Calendar of Close Rolls Edward III XI 302

The grant was probably in trust for Merton Priory, for in 1380 the prior was said to be holding the "manor" of Wickford; *VCH* IV (1912) 233, quoting 681 Inq. a.q.d. 395, No. 28.

4   *VCH* IV (1912) 233, quoting Valor Eccl. (Rec. Com.) ii, 48

5   *VCH* IV 231 quoting Pat. 36 Hen. VIII pt. xxvii

The Smythe Dynasty (1564–1725)

6   *Reliquary* 22/3 Note 49

7   *SyAC* II (1862) pt.II

The Smythe arms were amongst those of several notable families displayed in the west window of old Mitcham church. Manning and Bray II (1809) 500.

8   *Reliquary* 141 Note 28. The crest was incorporated in the inn sign of the eponymous *Buck's Head* at Fair Green Mitcham (renamed the *White Lion of Mortimer* in 1992) which was owned by the Smythes in the 17th century.

9   LMA – Bedford Estate Papers E/BER/S/T/II/B 3

(For this, and other references to the Smythes taken from the Bedford Papers, I am greatly indebted to Rita J Ensing of the Wandsworth Historical Society.)

10 Feet of Fines Surrey (*SyAC Extra Volume* 1 (1894))

11 BL Harl, 1. 433, fo. 186b.

12 Rowse A L, *The England of Elizabeth* (1955) 285

13 Or Elinora, née Hesilrigge, formerly of Leicestershire

14 *Reliquary* 141 Note 28 and
    Probate copy of will dated 6 Jan 1575/6, proved 1609/10, SHC 212/73/22

15 London County Council *Minutes of the Surrey and Kent Sewer Commissioners* (1909) 120

16 *VCH* IV (1912) 232

17 Smith E E F, *Clapham: an Historical Tour* 15

18 *Reliquary* 142-3 Note 31, which includes much detail from Clerk's will.
    I am indebted to Ray Ninnis, member of MHS, who kindly supplied information about the Clerks' monuments at Clapham.

19 *VCH* IV (1912) 231, quoting Feet of Fines Surrey, Easter 37, Elizabeth

20 Lay Subsidy Assessments 1593/4 *SyAC* XIX (1906) 42

21 SHC K77/4/1

22 Giuseppi M.S, 'The River Wandle in 1610' *SyAC* XXI (1908) 170-191

23 SHC – Survey of the Manor of Reigate, 46

24 Sir John Soane's Museum, Lincoln's Inn Fields – Adam Collection Vol 45 No 36

25 Berry W, *Surrey Genealogies* (1837)

26 LMA – E/BER/S/T/II/B/4

27 Montague E N, *Lower Green West, Mitcham* (MHS 2004) 102

28 SHC 212/113/ – deeds and mortgages 1645-1657

29 SHC 599/

30 SHC – plan in James Cranmer's Estate Book 1717

31 Montague E N, *Lower Mitcham* (MHS 2003) 36-7

32 SHC LA5/8/1-2 – Militia records

33 *Surrey Hearth Tax 1664* SyRS XVII (1940)

34 Parker E, *Surrey Anthology* (1952) 20

35 *SyAC* 39 (1938) 3 and 14

36 LMA – E/BER/S/T/II/B/10, 11 and 12

37 LMA – E/BER/S/T/II/B/32 and 14

The Myers Family (1715–1742)

38 SHC – Court Rolls of the Manor of Reigate

39 Ward W R (ed) *Parson and Parish in Eighteenth Century Surrey* (SyRS XXXIV 1994) 46

40 Prob. 11 604 162 (See Appendix 1a)

41 Prob. 11 719 226 (See Appendix 1b)

42 SHC – Court Rolls of the Manor of Biggin and Tamworth

43 *Alumni Oxoniensis* I 1003. William Myers junr. matriculated 10 June 1731, aged 18. He obtained his BA in 1735.

44 1721-1765

Scots at Mitcham Grove (1755-1786) – Archibald Stewart and Alexander Wedderburn

45 SHC – Mitcham Poor Rate Books.

46 Pottle F A *Boswell's London Journal 1762-1763* (1950, 1952) 236

47 *c.*1723-1781

48 Valentine A, *The British Establishment* II (1970) 826

49 Stewart seems to have married Arabella Ann Marlar, the daughter of John Marlar, a London merchant resident in Mitcham between 1782 and 1790.

50 SHC 303/21/4/1

51 Note dated October 1942

52 The National Trust *Claremont Landscape Garden* (1988) 21

53 Sir John Soane's Museum, Lincoln's Inn Fields. Adam Collection Vol.45 No. 36

54 Information from Hovis Ltd (Contained in notes appended to framed print of Mitcham Grove hanging in the cricket pavilion in 1974)

55 Miss Dawes cited as her sources:
Miss Avice Hoare of Godstone,
R Winder Esq, Archivist, Hoare's Bank, Fleet Street, EC4
SHC
TNA
Mitcham, Morden and Wimbledon Reference Libraries
DNB
Reliquary
Burke's *Landed Gentry*
Guide to St Nicholas Church, Godstone.
Hoare, Henry P.R. *Hoare's Bank, a Record 1672-1955. The Story of a Private Bank* (1955)
Sweet, James B, *A Memoir of the Late Henry Hoare, Esq, M.A.* (1869)
      (This Henry Hoare was a grandson of Henry of Mitcham)
Hutchinson, Horace G, *The Life of Sir John Lubbock, Lord Avebury* (1914)
Campbell, John, *Lives of the Lord Chancellors of England* Vol. 8 (1857)
Cooke's *Topography of Great Britain or The British Traveller's Pocket Directory* (1829).

Henry Hoare of Mitcham (1786–1828)

56 MLSC – Mitcham Vestry Minutes

57 Bidder H F (Ed), *Old Mitcham* (1923) article by R M Chart

58 Bryant A, *The Years of Endurance* (1944) 248, quoting Hannah More

59 MLSC – Mitcham Savings Bank records

60 Malcolm, James, *A Compendium of Modern Husbandry* III (1805) 397/8

61 1776-1819

62 Walford E, *Greater London – A Narrative of its History, its People, and Its Places* II (1898) 528

63 Jacques, J W, 'Godstone Rectors' *Surrey History* IV No. 3 (1990) 165

64 Lady Acland of Killerton, in a personal communication, 27 September 1992

Mitcham Grove – A Description

65 London Borough of Sutton Archives 2361/2/2 and Croydon Library HW904
    Particulars of the Sale by Auction of the Estate of Henry Hoare 1828

66 Hassell J, *Picturesque Walks and Rides* I (1817) 117/8

Mitcham Grove and the Lubbocks

67 Brayley IV (1850)

68 Morris J, 'The Anglo-Saxon Cemetery at Mitcham' *SyAC* LVI (1959) 51-131

8   GROVE HOUSE

1   It is shown, for instance, on Rocque's map of 1762.

2   SHC – Land Tax records

3   MLSC – Mitcham Vestry Minutes.

4   *VCH* II (1905) 371

5   Edwards II (1789) 18

6   London Borough of Sutton Archives 2361/2/2 and Croydon Library HW904
    Particulars of the Sale by Auction of the Estate of Henry Hoare 1828

7   Colvin H, *Biographical Dictionary of British Architects 1600-1840* (3rd
    ed 1995) 890-2

8   Mitcham Tithe – reference 1281: "House, garden etc." 1a. 3r. 5p.

9   Census returns 1851

10 *Green's South London Directory* (1869) 124: "Stanton J, mitcham grove"

11 Clark E F, *George Parker Bidder, The Calculating Boy* (1983) 115, 481 and
    information kindly supplied in personal correspondence

12 *VCH* IV (1912)

9   RAVENSBURY AND THE ORIGINS OF MITCHAM

1   Bidder and Morris 51-131

2   Slater

3   Adkins L, and Adkins R A, *Under the Sludge – Beddington Roman Villa*
    (1986)

4   NGR TQ 2607 6918 *SyAC* XLII (1934) 23-4

5   NGR TQ 2780 6750. (Willow Lane) *SyAC* XXXVIII part 1 (1929) 93 and
    XXXIX (1931) 45-6
    NGR TQ 274 691. (Mitcham Gas Works) *SyAC* XXXIX (1931) 146

6   NGR TQ 2673 6918. (Short Batsworth) Excavated by Denis Turner and
    members of Surrey Archaeological Society and local societies in 1965/6.
    Awaiting publication. Also Evaluation Report on excavations at Deen City
    Farm produced by the Museum of London Archaeology Service in 1993.

7   NGR TQ 2710 6785. *Surrey Archaeological Society Bulletin* 129. Excavation
    under direction of David Bird, 1974. Not yet published.

8   NGR TQ 2699 6857. Museum of London Archaeology Service Preliminary Report of Archaeological Evaluation Work at Benedict Road Primary School, Mitcham 1989.

9   'Grant by Frithewald, Subregulus of Surrey, and Bishop Erkenwald, of Moulsey and various other lands to Chertsey Abbey AD 727 (for 675)'. Birch W. de G, *Cartularium Saxonicum* I (1885) 64

10 For instance, Chalton, Hants, Bishopstone, Sussex, West Stow, Suffolk, and Mucking, Essex

11 Densem R, and Seeley D, 'Excavations at Rectory Grove, Clapham, 1980-81' in *The London Archaeologist* Vol. 4, No.7, 177-184

12 Morris J, 'Anglo-Saxon Surrey' in *SyAC* LVI (1959) 152

13 Gelling, M, *Signposts to the Past* (1978), comments that, admirable as they no doubt are, the early county volumes of the English Place Names Society, and Ekwall's *Concise Oxford Dictionary of English Places Names* are not wholly reliable, and the EPNS county volumes are being revised.

14 Gover *et al* 55

15 Gelling M, in *English Medieval Settlement* (Edited by Sawyer P H) (1979) 114

16 Gover *et al.* 52 list

Wicford	1199 FF(p)
Wikeford(e)	1200 Cur 1219 FF 1241 Ass
Wikford	1229 FF
Wycford	1242 Fees(p)
Wickford	1279 Ass
Wykford	c1280 BL

17 *Calendar of Close Rolls* X (1908) Edward XI 302
    VCH IV (1912) 233, quoting 68 Inq. a.d. 395, No. 28

18 Gelling M, *Signposts to the Past* (1978) 67

19 *Ibid*, 118

20 Hearnshaw F JC, *The Place of Surrey in the History of England* (1936) 34, observes: "The site of 'Wibbandune' is in dispute. Wimbledon is generally assumed, e.g. by Camden and by Mr R. Neville in *SyAC* X p.276; Mr H. E. Malden argues for Wipsedone, on the heaths near Chobham;Mr D. C. Whimster suggests Wipley, near Worplesdon."

21 Bidder and Morris 131

22 Gover *et al*

APPENDIX 4

1   Bird D G, 'Merton: Mitcham Grove (TQ 271679)' Surrey Archaeological Society *Bulletin* 114 (1975), 3-4; reprinted *SyAC* LXXI (1977) 284-5

2   Bidder H F & Morris J, 'The Anglo-Saxon cemetery at Mitcham', *SyAC* LVI (1959) 51-131

3   Turner D J, 'S W London team', Surrey Archaeological Society *Bulletin* 118 (1975) 3

4   Orton C, *Mathematics in Archaeology* (London 1980)

5   Pers. comm. John Clark, Museum of London